DOVER · THRIFT · EDITIONS

English Romantic Poetry

AN ANTHOLOGY

EDITED BY
STANLEY APPELBAUM

DOVER PUBLICATIONS, INC.

Mineola, New York

DOVER THRIFT EDITIONS

GENERAL EDITOR: STANLEY APPELBAUM

Copyright

Bibliographical Note

English Romantic Poetry is a new anthology, first published by Dover Publications, Inc., in 1996.

International Standard Book Number: 0-486-29282-7

Manufactured in the United States of America
Dover Publications, Inc., 31 East 2nd Street, Mineola, N.Y. 11501

Introduction

MANY NEW TRENDS have been introduced into the course of English poetry since the Romantic era, but certain basic achievements and acquisitions of the Romantics, whether original with them or rehabilitated and brilliantly reaffirmed by them, have never again been relinquished by English-language authors. Even today the word poet conjures up the Romantic notion: an individualistic, inspired seer revealing his inmost thoughts in a spontaneous upwelling of emotion (rather than — as in the earlier eighteenth century, for instance — a pontificating moralist legislating for all of mankind in artfully crafted phraseology).

At the very end of the eighteenth century and the beginning of the nineteenth, a number of like-minded individuals (there was never literally a "Romantic school" with codified content and committee directives) — gleaning suggestions from such proto-Romantics of the preceding generation as the poets Thomas Gray, William Collins and Thomas Chatterton and the novelist Horace Walpole; and smitten with the longing for freedom inherent in the American colonies' fight for independence and the startling revolution in France — rebelled against the smug rationality and optimism of most of their predecessors.

Blake replaced the arid atheism or tepid deism of the encyclopedists and their disciples with a glowing new personal religion; turned the attention of his readers to the downtrodden and disinherited; and eschewed the elaborate formal ode in favor of simple hymn stanzas or his own vigorous type of Bible verses. The upheavals of the incipient Industrial Revolution are also reflected in his social thought.

Wordsworth, likewise using simple verse forms (although he also restored the sonnet and blank verse to their former glory), depicted the life of humble peasants and children (from within, on their own terms); transformed nature poetry from a bland description or a pretext for allegory into an awestruck acknowledgment of God's grandeur and its effect on the psyche; and celebrated the self, the individual mind and feelings, as hardly anyone had done previously.

Coleridge, a scholar familiar with the past achievements of English poetry and attuned to contemporary European trends (Romanticism was burgeoning in France and Germany as well), opened the sluice gates of the imagination, flooding his verse with fantasy, wonderment and even horror; tapped his own experiences with dreams and drugs; restored interest in the ballad literature of past centuries; voiced pessimism, doubt and mental unease in a manner that speaks directly to us nearly two centuries later.

Byron bequeathed to us his exoticism and spirit of adventure, his very "modern" cynicism and satirical wit, his deep dissatisfaction with the human condition. In his own handsome person, he was the Romantic poet par excellence: impulsive, bohemian, elegant, seductive.

Shelley replaced the pompous Roman influence of the Neoclassical era with a deeply felt, personally reinterpreted return to Greek ideals; enriched the language's poetic armory immeasurably with original meters and stanzas; made sensitivity and ecstasy the keynotes of his world view; and — in the repressive era of the Napoleonic Wars and the post-Waterloo authoritarian backlash — embodied the spirit of healthy revolt against the fetters of government and society.

Keats was another who reshaped the world of Greece in a meaningful new way, but he also contributed to what would become the typically Romantic infatuation with the Middle Ages; in his best works he raised English poetic diction to unparalleled heights; in both his brief life and his poems he fostered the quintessential Romantic themes of unattainable aspirations and the evanescence of bright visions.

The combination of these varied traits and trends comprises what is now known as Romanticism. The term itself was coined later in the nineteenth century to differentiate from the preceding "classical" generation what was by then recognized as a decidedly new and contrasting movement.

Only the six above-mentioned giants are included in this anthology. The staff of Dover Publications considered the major poet Robert Burns, often anthologized as a Romantic, to be too much of an earlier, essentially eighteenth-century figure; and it seemed better to offer large amounts of Blake, Wordsworth, Coleridge, Byron, Shelley and Keats (represented, for the most part, by unabridged poems, sometimes of considerable length) than to dilute the anthology by the inclusion of poets of lesser stature or reputation. The reader interested in a broader view of the entire era is urged to supplement the present volume with selections from Thomas Moore, Leigh Hunt, Thomas Love Peacock, Walter Savage Landor, Charles Lamb, Robert Southey, Thomas Campbell, Samuel Rogers, George Crabbe, Sir Walter Scott, Thomas Hood and especially the visionary peasant-poet John Clare. Major prose works of the era, besides those of Coleridge, include the novels of Scott, Mary Shelley and Jane Austen, the essays of Lamb and William Hazlitt and the writings of Thomas De Quincey.

In the present volume the six chosen poets appear in order of year of birth; in each case, the poems are arranged chronologically by and large (dates in the table of contents). An alphabetical list of titles and first lines appear at the end of the book. Following in this Introduction are brief individual surveys of the six poets, with biographical data and a conspectus of the works included here.

William Blake (1757–1827)

By far the oldest of the poets in this volume (although he outlived Keats, Shelley and Byron), Blake was basically outside the mainstream of English Romantic poetry. Not only were his major works self-published in small numbers, and thus not readily accessible: his radical ideas on politics, society, ethics and the conduct of life were so advanced as to isolate him as an eccentric; and his poetic expression, although partly based on such traditional models as hymn writing, seventeenth-century poetry and King James biblical verses, was audacious and visionary in the extreme. (Moreover, it should always be recalled that Blake was an artist by profession and that most of his works were illustrated by him in an indissoluble, mutually illuminating marriage of words and pictures.) Blake was thus virtually unknown in his own day except for small coteries, remained unfamiliar for the rest of the nineteenth century except to an occasional champion like Dante Gabriel Rossetti, and was not fully rediscovered and rehabilitated until a full century after his death.

Unlike all the other poets in the present volume, whose travels molded their character, Blake, the son of a London haberdasher, never ventured very far from his native city; but, like those others, he was liberal in politics, sensitive to the oppressive government measures of his day, favorably inspired by the American Revolutionary War and the French Revolution, and inimical to the often stifling rationality and smug optimism of the eighteenth century. Like those others, he also found a new voice in poetry, achieving remarkable results with the simplest means and restoring rich musicality to the language.

The present selection includes 15 excerpts from Blake's two most famous collections, *Songs of Innocence* and *Songs of Experience*, in which, with childhood as his theme — now carefree, now careworn — Blake contrasts two states of the human soul, most strikingly exemplified in the two allegorical animal poems, "The Lamb" (passive Christian innocence, the purity of its whiteness) and "The Tyger" (the glory of color, the savage confrontation of existence). Also included are: "How sweet I roam'd from field to field," one of the pure, euphonious lyrics of his earliest collection, *Poetical Sketches*; four selections from his later, more philosophical lyrics (*Songs and Ballads*); the complete text of his early prophetic work *The Book of Thel*, which, in other terms and in a totally different poetic form, shares the preoccupations of the *Songs of Innocence* and *Songs of Experience*; the "Proverbs of Hell" section from the satirical *Marriage of Heaven and Hell*, which questions the traditional evilness of Satan; the "Preludium" from *America a Prophecy*, a foretaste of Blake's later, complex personal mythology; and the fairly late piece "And did those feet in ancient time," from the long prophetic poem *Milton*, an excerpt which has been adopted as a hymn in England.

Blake's distinctive spelling and punctuation have been retained in the present selection. The thematic "editorial arrangement" of "Auguries of Innocence," which occurs in Blake's manuscript in the form of disconnected couplets, is by David Erdman.

William Wordsworth (1770–1850)

Probably the most influential in the long run of all the English Romantic poets, Wordsworth was recognized at once as speaking with a new poetic voice that was rejuvenating English literature. Moreover, his "religion" of nature provided the Romantics and their spiritual successors with one of their major abiding themes. The poet's boyhood in the rugged and picturesque Lake District of northwestern England instilled this love of nature in him, and left him lastingly quiet, brooding and introspective. His foreign travels began in 1790, when he undertook a walking tour with a friend through parts of France, Italy, Switzerland and Germany; soon thereafter he spent another year in France, observing the revolutionary nation at close hand.

In 1795 a legacy left him and his sister Dorothy free of their legal guardians, and they moved to Dorset, where they met Coleridge; in 1797 and 1798 the like-minded trio lived together in Somerset. The latter year was that of the first edition of *Lyrical Ballads*, the epoch-making volume to which Wordsworth and Coleridge both contributed (the poets remained great friends until 1810). After the threesome visited Germany in 1798/9, they all went back to the Lake District, where Wordsworth remained for the rest of his long life, becoming a civil servant (county revenue collector) in 1813. He never stopped writing poetry, and was named poet laureate in 1843, but by general consensus his finest work was done by 1806.

The present selection includes: two pieces from the 1798 *Lyrical Ballads*, the folksong-like "We Are Seven" (one of the many pieces in which the poet speaks the "language of the lower and middle classes") and the stately "Tintern Abbey," exemplifying his philosophical bent and his matchless use of flexible and rich blank verse; "Nutting," a foretaste of the later *Prelude*; four of the five poems concerning a mysterious, possibly imaginary Lucy ("Strange fits . . . ," "She dwelt . . . ," "I travelled . . ." and "A slumber . . ."); "Lucy Gray"; "My heart leaps up . . ."; "Resolution and Independence," a unique blending of philosophical ode and rustic character study; five of the splendid 1802 sonnets that proved to be the greatest in English since Milton; "The Solitary Reaper," part of *Memorials of a Tour in Scotland*; "She was a Phantom of delight"; "I wandered lonely as a cloud," perhaps the best-known of his brief nature poems; the "Ode to Duty"; two brief excerpts from the vast autobiographical poem *The Prelude*, in which the poet recounted the development of his mind (often considered his greatest work); the "Ode: Intimations of Immortality," generally considered his finest single effort; and several more brief pieces, including one of the most inspired works of his old age, the elegy on the death of the Scottish writer James Hogg, a self-educated poet and author of the unusual novel *The Private Memoirs and Confessions of a Justified Sinner*.

Wordsworth clearly succeeded in what his friend Coleridge described as his task: to "give the charm of novelty to things of every day . . . directing [the mind] to the loveliness and the wonders of the world before us."

Samuel Taylor Coleridge (1772–1834)

Poetry comprised a smaller portion of Coleridge's literary output than was the case of any other poet represented here. He wrote vast amounts of important literary criticism, social thought, philosophy and theology in prose, and his *Biographia Literaria* of 1817 is often considered his greatest and most influential work. But his poetry, the best of which was written in the short space between 1797 and 1803, was innovative in form and spirit, and includes two works that are generally judged to be among the finest in the English language: "The Rime of the Ancient Mariner" and "Kubla Khan."

Born in Devon, the son of a vicar and grammar-school headmaster, Coleridge was a voracious reader, especially fond of works of fantasy. In his twenties, stirred by the French Revolution, he lectured on social problems along with the poet Robert Southey in Bristol, and the two even planned to found a utopia in America (in connection with this scheme, Coleridge hastily married a woman he never really loved).

In 1795 Coleridge met Wordsworth, and the two shared their existence in Dorset, Somerset, Germany (on funds supplied by the Wedgwood family) and the Lake District (where Coleridge unsuccessfully wooed Wordsworth's sister-in-law) until a bitter quarrel in 1810. Afterward, Coleridge lived in London, where he gave popular lectures and nurtured younger talents (all three of the remaining poets in this anthology were indebted to his advice or example). For years Coleridge was an opium addict, and some of his poems reflect the anguish this caused.

The present selection begins with "This Lime-Tree Bower My Prison," an early example of one of Coleridge's specialties: freely moving, informal, conversational blank-verse musings which influenced Wordsworth in "Tintern Abbey" and numerous later works. "The Dungeon" and "The Rime of the Ancient Mariner" were both first published in the original 1798 edition of *Lyrical Ballads*, the epoch-making joint effort of Wordsworth and Coleridge. "The Rime of the Ancient Mariner" (reprinted uncut), more than any other single poem, exemplifies the influence of older anonymous British ballads on the English Romantic movement (note, as well, the reference to "Sir Patrick Spens" at the beginning of "Dejection: An Ode"); the killing of the albatross is a crime against the universal life principle, an important theme in all of Coleridge's thought. "On a Ruined House in a Romantic Country" is a fine example of his humor: "The House That Jack Built" rewritten as a wild Gothic tale. "Christabel," also reprinted in its entirety, is a major philosophical narrative, with elements of the uncanny German writings of the "Sturm und Drang" and early Romantic periods. "Frost at Midnight" is another fine example of a "conversation poem" in blank verse. "France: An Ode," written in long, complex rhyming stanzas, expresses Coleridge's disappointment with the aggressive turn taken by the French Revolution, no longer a guarantor of liberty. "Kubla Khan," based on a dream experience, has possibly been subjected to more interpretation than any other poem, a whole book having been devoted to its subconscious sources in Coleridge's reading. The strongly autobiographical "Dejection: An Ode" and "The Pains of Sleep" are as heartfelt as they are beautifully expressed.

George Gordon, Lord Byron (1788–1824)

In the nineteenth century, throughout Europe and America, Byron was the most admired and best known of all the poets in this volume. Indeed, he was *the* Romantic poet par excellence, thanks to his good looks, his public pose, his physical handicap (a clubfoot), his wide travels and eventful existence, his liberality in politics, his gloom and his hectic — and eclectic — sex life. *Childe Harold's Pilgrimage*, the source of the "Byronic hero," made the poet famous at the age of 24, and this self-tormenting, world-weary hero soon reappeared in the swashbuckling narrative poems of 1813 and 1814, such as "The Giaour" and "The Corsair" (the period of Byron's love affair with his half-sister Augusta). Today, Byron is more admired for his humor and the remarkable satirical vein first revealed in his earliest major poem, "English Bards and Scotch Reviewers" (1809), developed in his long Venetian narrative poem *Beppo* (1817) and brought to perfection in "The Vision of Judgment" (1821) and the unfinished epic *Don Juan* (begun in 1818).

In his attitude, Byron was basically an eighteenth-century classicist, with a great admiration for Pope; technically, he was far from innovative, often using the conventional meters and manner of convivial songs (as in "She walks in beauty," which was one of a number of poems specifically intended to be set to music and sung), or adopting Italian *ottava rima* (the stanza form of *Beppo* and *Don Juan*).

Byron grew up in Scotland until inheriting his title at the age of ten, when he moved to England. His first long trip, 1809–11, ranging across Europe as far as Turkey, resulted in a captivation with the Mediterranean and Aegean landscape and life-style, and gave him material for both *Childe Harold's Pilgrimage* and the later *Don Juan*. His marriage in 1815 was disastrous, and the following year he left England for good. For a while he joined Shelley and his circle near Geneva (the famous paean to liberty, "The Prisoner of Chillon," reprinted in its entirety here, dates from this sojourn). In 1817 he moved on to Italy, where, especially in Venice and Ravenna, he was involved in many romances, both light and serious. In 1821 he rejoined Shelley's group in and near Pisa. In 1823, he went to Greece to aid in that nation's struggle for independence from Turkey; he died of a fever there early in 1824.

The present volume contains brief but important excerpts from *Childe Harold's Pilgrimage* (the Waterloo sequence, the invocation to the ocean, and the famous lyrical interpolation "Adieu, adieu! my native shore") and from *Don Juan* (a discussion of the poem itself, a reflection on his contemporaries and rivals among English poets, and the lyrical interpolation "The isles of Greece"). Included, uncut, are a number of lyrics and songs from 1808 to 1817; "The Prisoner of Chillon"; the eerie blank-verse description of the end of the world, "Darkness"; and the introspective "On This Day I Complete My Thirty-sixth Year," written only a couple of months before the poet's death.

For a more complete appreciation of Byron, one should also read his verse plays (especially *Manfred*) and his (prose) letters, in which he reveals his personality most fully.

Percy Bysshe Shelley (1792–1822)

For many, Shelley remains the perfect Romantic: for his quest after truth and justice, for his unparalleled learning (Greco-Roman and otherwise) and breadth of scope (poems on love, politics, history and philosophy), for the dazzling variety and novelty of his meters and stanzas, for the exquisiteness of his diction and delicacy of his thought. The present selection is almost fully comprised of brief lyrics (except for the grandiose pastoral elegy on the death of Keats, the "Adonais" of 1821); the only item that is not an entire work in itself is the famous final chorus from the verse play *Hellas* (1821). But the reader is heartily referred to such distinctive longer poems as "Alastor" (1816), "Julian and Maddalo" (1819), "The Mask of Anarchy" (1819) and "Epipsychidion" (1821), and the long verse plays *Prometheus Unbound* (1820) and *The Cenci* (1820). Shelley also wrote novels and important essays.

The poet was born into a wealthy family of landed gentry in Sussex, but even as a boy he was alien to his surroundings, and suffered from bad health all his life. In 1811, his second year at Oxford, he was expelled for writing an atheistic pamphlet. In the same year he infuriated his father by marrying Harriet Westbrook, a tavern keeper's daughter. The pair lived in the Lake District, Ireland and Wales until Shelley left Harriet in 1814 to elope with Mary Wollstonecraft Godwin, daughter of the feminist Mary Wollstonecraft and the influential philosopher William Godwin. The poet and Mary were married in 1816, after Harriet's suicide, and later that year spent some time near Geneva, where they met Byron. Shelley and his wife left England permanently in 1818, living in various parts of Italy before settling in Pisa in 1821. Their love eventually cooled because of the death of two of their children and Shelley's unsatisfiable personality. Among their circle in Pisa were Edward Williams and his common-law wife Jane, with whom Shelley flirted (see the three poems to Jane in the present anthology); Williams was drowned along with Shelley when the poet's yacht went down in a squall in 1822.

The poems in this book are all from Shelley's peak period, 1816 until his death. They include some of the most famous poems in the English language: the sonnet "Ozymandias," the rebellious political provocations "Song to the Men of England" and "England in 1819," the "Ode to the West Wind," "The Indian Serenade," "The Cloud," "To a Skylark" and a number of others. "Adonais," which was influenced by Milton's

"Lycidas" and is considered by many to surpass even that towering model as an elegy to the dead, is reprinted here in its entirety.

Shelley's reputation has undergone enormous vicissitudes; he has frequently been called immature, and opinions of his craftsmanship have differed widely. But today he seems firmly established as one of the greatest masters of them all.

John Keats (1795–1821)

Probably no other English poet developed so rapidly as Keats, all of whose memorable work was written between 1815 and 1820, or fulfilled as much of his promise at such an early age — cut off prematurely by the tuberculosis from which both his mother and his younger brother had died. Of humble social status, the son of a London livery-stable manager, Keats became enamored of Greek mythology and other studies at school, but, orphaned, was compelled to apprentice himself to a surgeon at the age of 15; he later studied at London hospitals. By the age of 18 he was already trying his hand at poetry, and two years later wrote the first uniquely Keatsian poem, the sonnet "On first looking into Chapman's Homer." Within a year or two, although his finances were always precarious, he devoted himself totally to poetry, under the influence of the writer Leigh Hunt, who introduced him to a number of other literary luminaries. In 1817 Keats wrote the long poem in heroic couplets *Endymion*; in 1818 "Isabella," a narrative in *ottava rima* (an Italian stanza form that Byron had made popular in *Beppo* and *Don Juan*). The year 1819 was pivotal, not only for the beginning of the poet's romance with Fanny Brawne but also for his amazing list of achievements: the Miltonic blank-verse epic fragment *Hyperion*, "The Eve of St. Agnes" (a narrative in Spenserian stanzas), the ballad-like "La Belle Dame sans Merci," the narrative in heroic couplets "Lamia," most of the great sonnets and, especially, the great odes, in which he fashioned unique stanzas and reached a perfection of poetic diction and musicality that stands alone. In 1820, on his way to Rome in quest of a better climate — his own tuberculosis had manifested itself — Keats completed the sonnet "Bright star, would I were stedfast as thou art." He died in Rome in 1821. There is no truth to the legend, which Byron believed (see the excerpt from *Don Juan* on page 142), that Keats's death was caused or hastened by hostile reviews of his work in literary journals.

The present selection includes, uncut, all the great odes ("Ode to a Nightingale," "Ode on a Grecian Urn," "Ode to Psyche," "To Autumn" and "Ode on Melancholy"); the most famous sonnets (this was a form that, along with Wordsworth, Keats raised to new heights in the Romantic era); the long narrative poems "Isabella" and "The Eve of St. Agnes"; "La Belle Dame sans Merci"; and a variety of miscellaneous poems, some of them, such as "To J. H. Reynolds Esq." and "To Mrs. Reynolds's Cat," revealing the good humor and high spirits that were part of the poet's contradictory character — although his bad health and other misfortunes brought him face to face, more than any of the other poets included here, with the misery of human existence.

The longest poems, mentioned above, have been omitted for reasons of space, but should be read for a full appreciation of Keats, in addition to his letters, in which he discusses his literary goals and criteria as well as many personal concerns.

Contents

(The years in parentheses are those of composition, unless
pertaining to a specific publication.)

WILLIAM BLAKE *(1757–1827)*

"Songs of Innocence": Introduction

Piping down the valleys wild,
Piping songs of pleasant glee,
On a cloud I saw a child,
And he laughing said to me:

"Pipe a song about a Lamb!"
So I piped with merry chear.
"Piper, pipe that song again;"
So I piped, he wept to hear.

"Drop thy pipe, thy happy pipe;
Sing thy songs of happy chear:"
So I sung the same again,
While he wept with joy to hear.

"Piper, sit thee down and write
In a book, that all may read."
So he vanish'd from my sight,
And I pluck'd a hollow reed,

And I made a rural pen,
And I stain'd the water clear,
And I wrote my happy songs
Every child may joy to hear.

Holy Thursday

'Twas on a Holy Thursday, their innocent faces clean,
The children walking two & two, in red & blue & green,
Grey-headed beadles walk'd before, with wands as white as snow,
Till into the high dome of Paul's they like Thames' waters flow.

O what a multitude they seem'd, these flowers of London town!
Seated in companies they sit with radiance all their own.
The hum of multitudes was there, but multitudes of lambs,
Thousands of little boys & girls raising their innocent hands.

Now like a mighty wind they raise to heaven the voice of song,
Or like harmonious thunderings the seats of heaven among.
Beneath them sit the aged men, wise guardians of the poor;
Then cherish pity, lest you drive an angel from your door.

Nurse's Song

When the voices of children are heard on the green,
And laughing is heard on the hill,
My heart is at rest within my breast,
And everything else is still.

"Then come home, my children, the sun is gone down,
And the dews of night arise;
Come, come, leave off play, and let us away
Till the morning appears in the skies."

"No, no, let us play, for it is yet day,
And we cannot go to sleep;
Besides, in the sky the little birds fly,
And the hills are all cover'd with sheep."

"Well, well, go & play till the light fades away,
And then go home to bed."
The little ones leaped & shouted & laugh'd
And all the hills ecchoed.

The Little Black Boy

My mother bore me in the southern wild,
And I am black, but O! my soul is white;
White as an angel is the English child,
But I am black as if bereav'd of light.

My mother taught me underneath a tree,
And, sitting down before the heat of day,
She took me on her lap and kissed me,
And pointing to the east began to say:

"Look on the rising sun: there God does live,
And gives his light, and gives his heat away;
And flowers and trees and beasts and men recieve
Comfort in morning, joy in the noonday.

"And we are put on earth a little space,
That we may learn to bear the beams of love;
And these black bodies and this sunburnt face
Is but a cloud, and like a shady grove.

"For when our souls have learn'd the heat to bear,
The cloud will vanish; we shall hear his voice,
Saying: 'Come out from the grove, my love & care,
And round my golden tent like lambs rejoice.' "

Thus did my mother say, and kissed me;
And thus I say to little English boy.
When I from black and he from white cloud free,
And round the tent of God like lambs we joy,

I'll shade him from the heat, till he can bear
To lean in joy upon our father's knee;
And then I'll stand and stroke his silver hair,
And be like him, and he will then love me.

The Lamb

Little Lamb, who made thee?
Dost thou know who made thee?
Gave thee life & bid thee feed,
By the stream & o'er the mead;
Gave thee clothing of delight,
Softest clothing, wooly, bright;
Gave thee such a tender voice,
Making all the vales rejoice?
Little Lamb, who made thee?
Dost thou know who made thee?

Little Lamb, I'll tell thee,
Little Lamb, I'll tell thee:
He is called by thy name,
For he calls himself a Lamb.
He is meek & he is mild;
He became a little child.
I a child & thou a lamb.
We are called by his name.
Little Lamb, God bless thee!
Little Lamb, God bless thee!

"Songs of Experience": Introduction

Hear the voice of the Bard!
Who Present, Past, & Future, sees;
Whose ears have heard
The Holy Word
That walk'd among the ancient trees,

Calling the lapsed Soul,
And weeping in the evening dew;
That might controll
The starry pole,
And fallen, fallen light renew!

"O Earth, O Earth, return!
"Arise from out the dewy grass;
"Night is worn,
"And the morn
"Rises from the slumberous mass.

"Turn away no more;
"Why wilt thou turn away?
"The starry floor,
"The wat'ry shore,
"Is giv'n thee till the break of day."

Earth's Answer

Earth rais'd up her head
From the darkness dread & drear.
Her light fled,
Stony dread!
And her locks cover'd with grey despair.

"Prison'd on wat'ry shore,
"Starry Jealousy does keep my den:
"Cold and hoar,
"Weeping o'er,
"I hear the Father of the ancient men.

"Selfish father of men!
"Cruel, jealous, selfish fear!
"Can delight,
"Chain'd in night,
"The virgins of youth and morning bear?

"Does spring hide its joy
"When buds and blossoms grow?
"Does the sower
"Sow by night,
"Or the plowman in darkness plow?

"Break this heavy chain
"That does freeze my bones around.
"Selfish! vain!
"Eternal bane!
"That free Love with bondage bound."

The Clod and the Pebble

"Love seeketh not Itself to please,
"Nor for itself hath any care,
"But for another gives its ease,
"And builds a Heaven in Hell's despair."

So sang a little Clod of Clay
Trodden with the cattle's feet,
But a Pebble of the brook
Warbled out these metres meet:

"Love seeketh only Self to please,
"To bind another to Its delight,
"Joys in another's loss of ease,
"And builds a Hell in Heaven's despite."

The Chimney Sweeper

A little black thing among the snow,
Crying ' 'weep! 'weep!' in notes of woe!
"Where are thy father & mother? say?"
"They are both gone up to the church to pray.

"Because I was happy upon the heath,
"And smil'd among the winter's snow,
"They clothed me in the clothes of death,
"And taught me to sing the notes of woe.

"And because I am happy & dance & sing,
"They think they have done me no injury,
"And are gone to praise God & his Priest & King,
"Who make up a heaven of our misery."

The Sick Rose

O Rose, thou art sick!
The invisible worm
That flies in the night,
In the howling storm,

Has found out thy bed
Of crimson joy:
And his dark secret love
Does thy life destroy.

The Tyger

Tyger! Tyger! burning bright
In the forests of the night,
What immortal hand or eye
Could frame thy fearful symmetry?

In what distant deeps or skies
Burnt the fire of thine eyes?
On what wings dare he aspire?
What the hand dare sieze the fire?

And what shoulder, & what art,
Could twist the sinews of thy heart?
And when thy heart began to beat,
What dread hand? & what dread feet?

What the hammer? what the chain?
In what furnace was thy brain?
What the anvil? what dread grasp
Dare its deadly terrors clasp?

When the stars threw down their spears,
And water'd heaven with their tears,
Did he smile his work to see?
Did he who made the Lamb make thee?

Tyger! Tyger! burning bright
In the forests of the night,
What immortal hand or eye
Dare frame thy fearful symmetry?

Ah! Sun-Flower

Ah, Sun-flower, weary of time,
Who countest the steps of the Sun,
Seeking after that sweet golden clime
Where the traveller's journey is done:

Where the Youth pined away with desire,
And the pale Virgin shrouded in snow
Arise from their graves, and aspire
Where my Sun-flower wishes to go.

The Garden of Love

I went to the Garden of Love,
And saw what I never had seen:
A Chapel was built in the midst,
Where I used to play on the green.

And the gates of this Chapel were shut,
And "Thou shalt not" writ over the door;
So I turn'd to the Garden of Love
That so many sweet flowers bore;

And I saw it was filled with graves,
And tomb-stones where flowers should be;
And Priests in black gowns were walking their rounds,
And binding with briars my joys & desires.

London

I wander thro' each charter'd street,
Near where the charter'd Thames does flow,
And mark in every face I meet
Marks of weakness, marks of woe.

In every cry of every Man,
In every Infant's cry of fear,
In every voice, in every ban,
The mind-forg'd manacles I hear.

How the Chimney-sweeper's cry
Every black'ning Church appalls;
And the hapless Soldier's sigh
Runs in blood down Palace walls.

But most thro' midnight streets I hear
How the youthful Harlot's curse
Blasts the new born Infant's tear,
And blights with plagues the Marriage hearse.

A Poison Tree

I was angry with my friend:
I told my wrath, my wrath did end.
I was angry with my foe:
I told it not, my wrath did grow.

And I water'd it in fears,
Night & morning with my tears;
And I sunned it with smiles,
And with soft deceitful wiles.

And it grew both day and night,
Till it bore an apple bright;
And my foe beheld it shine,
And he knew that it was mine,

And into my garden stole
When the night had veil'd the pole:
In the morning glad I see
My foe outstretch'd beneath the tree.

Song

How sweet I roam'd from field to field,
    And tasted all the summer's pride,
'Till I the prince of love beheld,
    Who in the sunny beams did glide!

He shew'd me lilies for my hair,
    And blushing roses for my brow;
He led me through his gardens fair,
    Where all his golden pleasures grow.

With sweet May dews my wings were wet,
    And Phoebus fir'd my vocal rage;
He caught me in his silken net,
    And shut me in his golden cage.

He loves to sit and hear me sing,
    Then, laughing, sports and plays with me;
Then stretches out my golden wing,
    And mocks my loss of liberty.

"I saw a chapel all of gold"

I saw a chapel all of gold
That none did dare to enter in
And many weeping stood without
Weeping mourning worshipping

I saw a serpent rise between
The white pillars of the door
And he forcd & forcd & forcd
Down the golden hinges tore

And along the pavement sweet
Set with pearls & rubies bright
All his slimy length he drew
Till upon the altar white

Vomiting his poison out
On the bread & on the wine
So I turnd into a sty
And laid me down among the swine

"Mock on, mock on, Voltaire, Rousseau"

Mock on Mock on Voltaire Rousseau
Mock on Mock on! tis all in vain!
You throw the sand against the wind
And the wind blows it back again

And every sand becomes a Gem
Reflected in the beams divine
Blown back they blind the mocking Eye
But still in Israels paths they shine

The Atoms of Democritus
And Newtons Particles of light
Are sands upon the Red sea shore
Where Israels tents do shine so bright

The Smile

There is a Smile of Love
And there is a Smile of Deceit
And there is a Smile of Smiles
In which these two Smiles meet

And there is a Frown of Hate
And there is a Frown of Disdain
And there is a Frown of Frowns
Which you strive to forget in vain

For it sticks in the Hearts deep Core
And it sticks in the deep Back bone
And no Smile that ever was smild
But only one Smile alone

That betwixt the Cradle & Grave
It only once Smild can be
But when it once is Smild
Theres an end to all Misery

Auguries of Innocence

[AS REARRANGED FROM THE MANUSCRIPT BY DAVID ERDMAN]

To see a World in a Grain of Sand
And a Heaven in a Wild Flower
Hold Infinity in the palm of your hand
And Eternity in an hour

A Robin Red breast in a Cage
Puts all Heaven in a Rage
A Dove house filld with Doves & Pigeons
Shudders Hell thro all its regions
A dog starvd at his Masters Gate
Predicts the ruin of the State
A Horse misusd upon the Road
Calls to Heaven for Human blood
Each outcry of the hunted Hare
A fibre from the Brain does tear
A Skylark wounded in the wing
A Cherubim does cease to sing
The Game Cock clipd & armd for fight
Does the Rising Sun affright
The Lamb misusd breeds Public Strife
And yet forgives the Butchers Knife
He who shall train the Horse to War
Shall never pass the Polar Bar

Every Wolfs & Lions howl
Raises from Hell a Human Soul
The Bleat the Bark Bellow & Roar
Are Waves that Beat on Heavens Shore
The wild deer wandring here & there
Keeps the Human Soul from Care
The Beggers Dog & Widows Cat
Feed them & thou wilt grow fat
He who shall hurt the little Wren
Shall never be belovd by Men
He who the Ox to wrath has movd
Shall never be by Woman lovd
He who torments the Chafers sprite
Weaves a Bower in endless Night
The wanton Boy that kills the Fly
Shall feel the Spiders enmity
The Catterpiller on the Leaf
Repeats to thee thy Mothers grief
Kill not the Moth nor Butterfly
For the Last Judgment draweth nigh
The Bat that flits at close of Eve
Has left the Brain that wont Believe
The Owl that calls upon the Night
Speaks the Unbelievers fright
The Gnat that sings his Summers song
Poison gets from Slanders tongue
The poison of the Snake & Newt
Is the sweat of Envys Foot
The Poison of the Honey Bee
Is the Artists Jealousy
A Riddle or the Crickets Cry
Is to Doubt a fit Reply
The Emmets Inch & Eagles Mile
Make Lame Philosophy to smile
He who Doubts from what he sees
Will neer Believe do what you Please
If the Sun & Moon should Doubt
Theyd immediately Go out
He who mocks the Infants Faith
Shall be mock'd in Age & Death
He who shall teach the Child to Doubt
The rotting Grave shall neer get out

He who respects the Infants faith
Triumphs over Hell & Death
The Childs Toys & the Old Mans Reasons
Are the Fruits of the Two seasons
The Questioner who sits so sly
Shall never know how to Reply
He who replies to words of Doubt
Doth put the Light of Knowledge out
A Truth thats told with bad intent
Beats all the Lies you can invent
Joy & Woe are woven fine
A Clothing for the Soul divine
Under every grief & pine
Runs a joy with silken twine
It is right it should be so
Man was made for Joy & Woe
And when this we rightly know
Thro the World we safely go
The Babe is more than swadling Bands
Throughout all these Human Lands
Tools were made & Born were hands
Every Farmer Understands
Every Tear from Every Eye
Becomes a Babe in Eternity
This is caught by Females bright
And returnd to its own delight
The Babe that weeps the Rod beneath
Writes Revenge in realms of Death
The Princes Robes & Beggars Rags
Are Toadstools on the Misers Bags
The Beggars Rags fluttering in Air
Does to Rags the Heavens tear
The poor Mans Farthing is worth more
Than all the Gold on Africs Shore
One Mite wrung from the Labrers hands
Shall buy & sell the Misers Lands
Or if protected from on high
Does that whole Nation sell & buy
The Strongest Poison ever known
Came from Caesars Laurel Crown
Nought can Deform the Human Race
Like to the Armours iron brace

The Soldier armd with Sword & Gun
Palsied strikes the Summers Sun
When Gold & Gems adorn the Plow
To peaceful Arts shall Envy Bow
To be in a Passion you Good may Do
But no Good if a Passion is in you
The Whore & Gambler by the State
Licencd build that Nations Fate
The Harlots cry from Street to Street
Shall weave Old Englands winding Sheet
The Winners Shout the Losers Curse
Dance before dead Englands Hearse
Every Night & every Morn
Some to Misery are Born
Every Morn & every Night
Some are Born to sweet delight
Some are Born to sweet delight
Some are Born to Endless Night
We are led to Believe a Lie
When we see not Thro the Eye
Which was Born in a Night to perish in a Night
When the Soul Slept in Beams of Light
God Appears & God is Light
To those poor Souls who dwell in Night
But does a Human Form Display
To those who Dwell in Realms of day

The Book of Thel

THEL'S MOTTO

Does the Eagle know what is in the pit?
Or wilt thou go ask the Mole:
Can Wisdom be put in a silver rod?
Or Love in a golden bowl?

THEL

I

The daughters of Mne Seraphim led round their sunny flocks.
All but the youngest; she in paleness sought the secret air.

To fade away like morning beauty from her mortal day:
Down by the river of Adona her soft voice is heard:
And thus her gentle lamentation falls like morning dew.

O life of this our spring! why fades the lotus of the water?
Why fade these children of the spring? born but to smile & fall.
Ah! Thel is like a watry bow, and like a parting cloud.
Like a reflection in a glass. like shadows in the water.
Like dreams of infants. like a smile upon an infants face,
Like the doves voice, like transient day, like music in the air;
Ah! gentle may I lay me down, and gentle rest my head.
And gentle sleep the sleep of death. and gentle hear the voice
Of him that walketh in the garden in the evening time.

The Lilly of the valley breathing in the humble grass
Answer'd the lovely maid and said; I am a watry weed,
And I am very small, and love to dwell in lowly vales;
So weak, the gilded butterfly scarce perches on my head.
Yet I am visited from heaven and he that smiles on all.
Walks in the valley. and each morn over me spreads his hand
Saying, rejoice thou humble grass, thou new-born lilly flower,
Thou gentle maid of silent valleys. and of modest brooks;
For thou shalt be clothed in light, and fed with morning manna:
Till summers heat melts thee beside the fountains and the springs
To flourish in eternal vales: then why should Thel complain,
Why should the mistress of the vales of Har, utter a sigh.

She ceasd & smild in tears, then sat down in her silver shrine.

Thel answerd. O thou little virgin of the peaceful valley.
Giving to those that cannot crave, the voiceless, the o'ertired.
Thy breath doth nourish the innocent lamb, he smells thy milky
    garments,
He crops thy flowers. while thou sittest smiling in his face,
Wiping his mild and meekin mouth from all contagious taints.
Thy wine doth purify the golden honey, thy perfume,
Which thou dost scatter on every little blade of grass that springs
Revives the milked cow, & tames the fire-breathing steed.
But Thel is like a faint cloud kindled at the rising sun:
I vanish from my pearly throne, and who shall find my place.

Queen of the vales the Lilly answerd, ask the tender cloud,
And it shall tell thee why it glitters in the morning sky,
And why it scatters its bright beauty thro' the humid air.
Descend O little cloud & hover before the eyes of Thel.

The Cloud descended, and the Lilly bowd her modest head:
And went to mind her numerous charge among the verdant grass.

II

O little Cloud the virgin said, I charge thee tell to me,
Why thou complainest not when in one hour thou fade away:
Then we shall seek thee but not find; ah Thel is like to thee.
I pass away. yet I complain, and no one hears my voice.

The Cloud then shew'd his golden head & his bright form emerg'd,
Hovering and glittering on the air before the face of Thel.

O virgin know'st thou not. our steeds drink of the golden springs
Where Luvah doth renew his horses: look'st thou on my youth,
And fearest thou because I vanish and am seen no more.
Nothing remains; O maid I tell thee, when I pass away,
It is to tenfold life, to love, to peace, and raptures holy:
Unseen descending, weigh my light wings upon balmy flowers;
And court the fair eyed dew. to take me to her shining tent;
The weeping virgin, trembling kneels before the risen sun,
Till we arise link'd in a golden band, and never part;
But walk united, bearing food to all our tender flowers

Dost thou O little Cloud? I fear that I am not like thee;
For I walk through the vales of Har. and smell the sweetest flowers;
But I feed not the little flowers: I hear the warbling birds,
But I feed not the warbling birds. they fly and seek their food;
But Thel delights in these no more because I fade away,
And all shall say, without a use this shining woman liv'd,
Or did she only live. to be at death the food of worms.

The Cloud reclind upon his airy throne and answer'd thus.

Then if thou art the food of worms. O virgin of the skies,
How great thy use. how great thy blessing; every thing that lives,
Lives not alone, nor for itself: fear not and I will call
The weak worm from its lowly bed, and thou shalt hear its voice.
Come forth worm of the silent valley, to thy pensive queen.

The helpless worm arose, and sat upon the Lillys leaf,
And the bright Cloud saild on, to find his partner in the vale.

III

Then Thel astonish'd view'd the Worm upon its dewy bed.

Art thou a Worm? image of weakness. art thou but a Worm?
I see thee like an infant wrapped in the Lillys leaf:
Ah weep not little voice, thou can'st not speak. but thou can'st weep;
Is this a Worm? I see thee lay helpless & naked: weeping,
And none to answer, none to cherish thee with mothers smiles.

The Clod of Clay heard the Worms voice, & raisd her pitying head;
She bow'd over the weeping infant, and her life exhal'd
In milky fondness, then on Thel she fix'd her humble eyes.

O beauty of the vales of Har. we live not for ourselves,
Thou seest me the meanest thing, and so I am indeed;
My bosom of itself is cold. and of itself is dark,
But he that loves the lowly, pours his oil upon my head.
And kisses me, and binds his nuptial bands around my breast.
And says; Thou mother of my children, I have loved thee.
And I have given thee a crown that none can take away
But how this is sweet maid, I know not, and I cannot know,
I ponder, and I cannot ponder; yet I live and love.

The daughter of beauty wip'd her pitying tears with her white veil,
And said. Alas! I knew not this, and therefore did I weep:
That God would love a Worm I knew, and punish the evil foot
That wilful, bruis'd its helpless form: but that he cherish'd it
With milk and oil, I never knew; and therefore did I weep,
And I complaind in the mild air, because I fade away,
And lay me down in thy cold bed, and leave my shining lot.
Queen of the vales, the matron Clay answerd; I heard thy sighs.
And all thy moans flew o'er my roof. but I have call'd them down:
Wilt thou O Queen enter my house. 'tis given thee to enter,
And to return; fear nothing. enter with thy virgin feet.

IV

The eternal gates terrific porter lifted the northern bar:
Thel enter'd in & saw the secrets of the land unknown;
She saw the couches of the dead, & where the fibrous roots

Of every heart on earth infixes deep its restless twists:
A land of sorrows & of tears where never smile was seen.

She wanderd in the land of clouds thro' valleys dark, listning
Dolours & lamentations: waiting oft beside a dewy grave
She stood in silence. listning to the voices of the ground,
Till to her own grave plot she came, & there she sat down.
And heard this voice of sorrow breathed from the hollow pit.

Why cannot the Ear be closed to its own destruction?
Or the glistning Eye to the poison of a smile!
Why are Eyelids stord with arrows ready drawn,
Where a thousand fighting men in ambush lie?
Or an Eye of gifts & graces, show'ring fruits & coined gold!
Why a Tongue impress'd with honey from every wind?
Why an Ear, a whirlpool fierce to draw creations in?
Why a Nostril wide inhaling terror trembling & affright.
Why a tender curb upon the youthful burning boy!
Why a little curtain of flesh on the bed of our desire?

The Virgin started from her seat, & with a shriek.
Fled back unhinderd till she came into the vales of Har

Proverbs of Hell

In seed time learn, in harvest teach, in winter enjoy.

Drive your cart and your plow over the bones of the dead.
The road of excess leads to the palace of wisdom.

Prudence is a rich ugly old maid courted by Incapacity.
He who desires but acts not, breeds pestilence.

The cut worm forgives the plow.

Dip him in the river who loves water.

A fool sees not the same tree that a wise man sees.
He whose face gives no light, shall never become a star.
Eternity is in love with the productions of time.
The busy bee has no time for sorrow.
The hours of folly are measur'd by the clock, but of wisdom: no clock
    can measure.

All wholsom food is caught without a net or a trap.
Bring out number weight & measure in a year of dearth.

No bird soars too high. if he soars with his own wings.

A dead body. revenges not injuries.

The most sublime act is to set another before you.

If the fool would persist in his folly he would become wise
Folly is the cloke of knavery.

Shame is Prides cloke.

Prisons are built with stones of Law, Brothels with bricks of Religion.
The pride of the peacock is the glory of God.
The lust of the goat is the bounty of God.
The wrath of the lion is the wisdom of God.
The nakedness of woman is the work of God.

Excess of sorrow laughs. Excess of joy weeps.

The roaring of lions, the howling of wolves, the raging of the stormy sea,
    and the destructive sword. are portions of eternity too great for the
    eye of man.

The fox condemns the trap, not himself.

Joys impregnate. Sorrows bring forth.

Let man wear the fell of the lion. woman the fleece of the sheep.

The bird a nest, the spider a web, man friendship.

The selfish smiling fool. & the sullen frowning fool. shall be both
    thought wise. that they may be a rod.

What is now proved was once, only imagin'd.
The rat, the mouse, the fox, the rabbet; watch the roots, the lion, the
    tyger, the horse, the elephant, watch the fruits.

The cistern contains: the fountain overflows

One thought. fills immensity.
Always be ready to speak your mind, and a base man will avoid you.

Every thing possible to be believ'd is an image of truth.

The eagle never lost so much time. as when he submitted to learn of the
    crow.

The fox provides for himself. but God provides for the lion.

Think in the morning, Act in the noon, Eat in the evening, Sleep in the
night.

He who has sufferd you to impose on him knows you.

As the plow follows words, so God rewards prayers.

The tygers of wrath are wiser than the horses of instruction

Expect poison from the standing water.

You never know what is enough unless you know what is more than
enough.

Listen to the fools reproach! it is a kingly title!

The eyes of fire, the nostrils of air, the mouth of water, the beard of earth.

The weak in courage is strong in cunning.

The apple tree never asks the beech how he shall grow, nor the lion. the
horse; how he shall take his prey.

The thankful reciever bears a plentiful harvest.

If others had not been foolish. we should be so.

The soul of sweet delight. can never be defil'd,

When thou seest an Eagle, thou seest a portion of Genius. lift up thy
head!

As the catterpiller chooses the fairest leaves to lay her eggs on, so the
priest lays his curse on the fairest joys,

To create a little flower is the labour of ages.

Damn. braces: Bless relaxes.

The best wine is the oldest. the best water the newest.

Prayers plow not! Praises reap not!

Joys laugh not! Sorrows weep not!

The head Sublime, the heart Pathos, the genitals Beauty, the hands &
feet Proportion.

As the air to a bird or the sea to a fish, so is contempt to the contemptible.

The crow wish'd every thing was black, the owl, that every thing was
white.

Exuberance is Beauty.

If the lion was advised by the fox. he would be cunning.

Improvement makes strait roads, but the crooked roads without Improvement, are roads of Genius.

Sooner murder an infant in its cradle than nurse unacted desires

Where man is not nature is barren.

Truth can never be told so as to be understood, and not be believ'd.

Enough! or Too much

"America a Prophecy": Preludium

The shadowy daughter of Urthona stood before red Orc.
When fourteen suns had faintly journey'd o'er his dark abode;
His food she brought in iron baskets, his drink in cups of iron;
Crown'd with a helmet & dark hair the nameless female stood;
A quiver with its burning stores, a bow like that of night,
When pestilence is shot from heaven; no other arms she need:
Invulnerable tho' naked, save where clouds roll round her loins,
Their awful folds in the dark air; silent she stood as night;
For never from her iron tongue could voice or sound arise;
But dumb till that dread day when Orc assay'd his fierce embrace.

Dark virgin; said the hairy youth, thy father stern abhorr'd;
Rivets my tenfold chains while still on high my spirit soars;
Sometimes an eagle screaming in the sky, sometimes a lion,
Stalking upon the mountains, & sometimes a whale I lash
The raging fathomless abyss, anon a serpent folding
Around the pillars of Urthona, and round thy dark limbs,
On the Canadian wilds I fold, feeble my spirit folds.
For chaind beneath I rend these caverns; when thou bringest food
I howl my joy! and my red eyes seek to behold thy face
In vain! these clouds roll to & fro, & hide thee from my sight.

Silent as despairing love, and strong as jealousy,
The hairy shoulders rend the links, free are the wrists of fire;
Round the terrific loins he siez'd the panting struggling womb;
It joy'd: she put aside her clouds & smiled her first-born smile;
As when a black cloud shews its light'nings to the silent deep.

Soon as she saw the terrible boy then burst the virgin cry.

I know thee, I have found thee, & I will not let thee go;
Thou art the image of God who dwells in darkness of Africa;

And thou art fall'n to give me life in regions of dark death.
On my American plains I feel the struggling afflictions
Endur'd by roots that writhe their arms into the nether deep:
I see a serpent in Canada, who courts me to his love;
In Mexico an Eagle, and a Lion in Peru;
I see a Whale in the South-sea, drinking my soul away.
O what limb rending pains I feel. thy fire & my frost
Mingle in howling pains, in furrows by thy lightnings rent;
This is eternal death; and this the torment long foretold.

"And did those feet in ancient time"

And did those feet in ancient time,
Walk upon Englands mountains green:
And was the holy Lamb of God,
On Englands pleasant pastures seen!

And did the Countenance Divine,
Shine forth upon our clouded hills?
And was Jerusalem builded here,
Among these dark Satanic Mills?

Bring me my Bow of burning gold:
Bring me my Arrows of desire:
Bring me my Spear: O clouds unfold!
Bring me my Chariot of fire!

I will not cease from Mental Fight,
Nor shall my Sword sleep in my hand:
Till we have built Jerusalem,
In Englands green & pleasant Land.

WILLIAM WORDSWORTH *(1770–1850)*

We Are Seven

 —— A simple Child,
That lightly draws its breath,
And feels its life in every limb,
What should it know of death?

I met a little cottage Girl:
She was eight years old, she said;
Her hair was thick with many a curl
That clustered round her head.

She had a rustic, woodland air,
And she was wildly clad:
Her eyes were fair, and very fair;
— Her beauty made me glad.

"Sisters and brothers, little Maid,
How many may you be?"
"How many? Seven in all," she said
And wondering looked at me.

"And where are they? I pray you tell."
She answered, "Seven are we;
And two of us at Conway dwell,
And two are gone to sea.

"Two of us in the church-yard lie,
My sister and my brother;
And, in the church-yard cottage, I
Dwell near them with my mother."

"You say that two at Conway dwell,
And two are gone to sea,
Yet ye are seven! — I pray you tell,
Sweet Maid, how this may be."

Then did the little Maid reply,
"Seven boys and girls are we;
Two of us in the church-yard lie,
Beneath the church-yard tree."

"You run about, my little Maid,
Your limbs they are alive;
If two are in the church-yard laid,
Then ye are only five."

"Their graves are green, they may be seen,"
The little Maid replied,
"Twelve steps or more from my mother's door,
And they are side by side.

"My stockings there I often knit,
My kerchief there I hem;
And there upon the ground I sit,
And sing a song to them.

"And often after sunset, Sir,
When it is light and fair,
I take my little porringer,
And eat my supper there.

"The first that died was sister Jane;
In bed she moaning lay,
Till God released her of her pain;
And then she went away.

"So in the church-yard she was laid;
And, when the grass was dry,
Together round her grave we played,
My brother John and I.

"And when the ground was white with snow,
And I could run and slide,
My brother John was forced to go,
And he lies by her side."

"How many are you, then," said I,
"If they two are in heaven?"
Quick was the little Maid's reply,
"O Master! we are seven."

"But they are dead; those two are dead!
Their spirits are in heaven!"
'T was throwing words away; for still
The little Maid would have her will,
And said, "Nay, we are seven!"

Lines

COMPOSED A FEW MILES ABOVE
TINTERN ABBEY, ON REVISITING
THE BANKS OF THE WYE
DURING A TOUR. JULY 13, 1798

Five years have past; five summers, with the length
Of five long winters! and again I hear
These waters, rolling from their mountain-springs
With a soft inland murmur. — Once again
Do I behold these steep and lofty cliffs,
That on a wild secluded scene impress
Thoughts of more deep seclusion; and connect
The landscape with the quiet of the sky.
The day is come when I again repose
Here, under this dark sycamore, and view
These plots of cottage-ground, these orchard-tufts,
Which at this season, with their unripe fruits,
Are clad in one green hue, and lose themselves
'Mid groves and copses. Once again I see
These hedge-rows, hardly hedge-rows, little lines
Of sportive wood run wild: these pastoral farms,
Green to the very door; and wreaths of smoke
Sent up, in silence, from among the trees!
With some uncertain notice, as might seem
Of vagrant dwellers in the houseless woods,

Or of some Hermit's cave, where by his fire
The Hermit sits alone.
              These beauteous forms,
Through a long absence, have not been to me
As is a landscape to a blind man's eye:
But oft, in lonely rooms, and 'mid the din
Of towns and cities, I have owed to them
In hours of weariness, sensations sweet,
Felt in the blood, and felt along the heart;
And passing even into my purer mind,
With tranquil restoration: — feelings too
Of unremembered pleasure: such, perhaps,
As have no slight or trivial influence
On that best portion of a good man's life,
His little, nameless, unremembered, acts
Of kindness and of love. Nor less, I trust,
To them I may have owed another gift,
Of aspect more sublime; that blessed mood,
In which the burthen of the mystery,
In which the heavy and the weary weight
Of all this unintelligible world,
Is lightened: — that serene and blessed mood,
In which the affections gently lead us on, —
Until, the breath of this corporeal frame
And even the motion of our human blood
Almost suspended, we are laid asleep
In body, and become a living soul:
While with an eye made quiet by the power
Of harmony, and the deep power of joy,
We see into the life of things.
                  If this
Be but a vain belief, yet, oh! how oft —
In darkness and amid the many shapes
Of joyless daylight; when the fretful stir
Unprofitable, and the fever of the world,
Have hung upon the beatings of my heart —
How oft, in spirit, have I turned to thee,
O sylvan Wye! thou wanderer thro' the woods,
How often has my spirit turned to thee!
    And now, with gleams of half-extinguished thought,
With many recognitions dim and faint,
And somewhat of a sad perplexity,
The picture of the mind revives again:

While here I stand, not only with the sense
Of present pleasure, but with pleasing thoughts
That in this moment there is life and food
For future years. And so I dare to hope,
Though changed, no doubt, from what I was when first
I came among these hills; when like a roe
I bounded o'er the mountains, by the sides
Of the deep rivers, and the lonely streams,
Wherever nature led: more like a man
Flying from something that he dreads, than one
Who sought the thing he loved. For nature then
(The coarser pleasures of my boyish days,
And their glad animal movements all gone by)
To me was all in all. — I cannot paint
What then I was. The sounding cataract
Haunted me like a passion: the tall rock,
The mountain, and the deep and gloomy wood,
Their colours and their forms, were then to me
An appetite; a feeling and a love,
That had no need of a remoter charm,
By thought supplied, nor any interest
Unborrowed from the eye. — That time is past,
And all its aching joys are now no more,
And all its dizzy raptures. Not for this
Faint I, nor mourn nor murmur; other gifts
Have followed; for such loss, I would believe,
Abundant recompense. For I have learned
To look on nature, not as in the hour
Of thoughtless youth; but hearing often-times
The still, sad music of humanity,
Nor harsh nor grating, though of ample power
To chasten and subdue. And I have felt
A presence that disturbs me with the joy
Of elevated thoughts; a sense sublime
Of something far more deeply interfused,
Whose dwelling is the light of setting suns,
And the round ocean and the living air,
And the blue sky, and in the mind of man;
A motion and a spirit, that impels
All thinking things, all objects of all thought,
And rolls through all things. Therefore am I still
A lover of the meadows and the woods,
And mountains; and of all that we behold

From this green earth; of all the mighty world
Of eye, and ear, — both what they half create,
And what perceive; well pleased to recognise
In nature and the language of the sense,
The anchor of my purest thoughts, the nurse,
The guide, the guardian of my heart, and soul
Of all my moral being.
                Nor perchance,
If I were not thus taught, should I the more
Suffer my genial spirits to decay:
For thou art with me here upon the banks
Of this fair river; thou my dearest Friend,
My dear, dear Friend; and in thy voice I catch
The language of my former heart, and read
My former pleasures in the shooting lights
Of thy wild eyes. Oh! yet a little while
May I behold in thee what I was once,
My dear, dear Sister! and this prayer I make,
Knowing that Nature never did betray
The heart that loved her; 'tis her privilege,
Through all the years of this our life, to lead
From joy to joy: for she can so inform
The mind that is within us, so impress
With quietness and beauty, and so feed
With lofty thoughts, that neither evil tongues,
Rash judgments, nor the sneers of selfish men,
Nor greetings where no kindness is, nor all
The dreary intercourse of daily life,
Shall e'er prevail against us, or disturb
Our cheerful faith, that all which we behold
Is full of blessings. Therefore let the moon
Shine on thee in thy solitary walk;
And let the misty mountain-winds be free
To blow against thee: and, in after years,
When these wild ecstasies shall be matured
Into a sober pleasure; when thy mind
Shall be a mansion for all lovely forms,
Thy memory be as a dwelling-place
For all sweet sounds and harmonies; oh! then,
If solitude, or fear, or pain, or grief,
Should be thy portion, with what healing thoughts
Of tender joy wilt thou remember me,

And these my exhortations! Nor, perchance —
If I should be where I no more can hear
Thy voice, nor catch from thy wild eyes these gleams
Of past existence — wilt thou then forget
That on the banks of this delightful stream
We stood together; and that I, so long
A worshipper of Nature, hither came
Unwearied in that service: rather say
With warmer love — oh! with far deeper zeal
Of holier love. Nor wilt thou then forget,
That after many wanderings, many years
Of absence, these steep woods and lofty cliffs,
And this green pastoral landscape, were to me
More dear, both for themselves and for thy sake!

Nutting

       —— It seems a day
(I speak of one from many singled out)
One of those heavenly days that cannot die;
When, in the eagerness of boyish hope,
I left our cottage-threshold, sallying forth
With a huge wallet o'er my shoulders slung,
A nutting-crook in hand; and turned my steps
Tow'rd some far-distant wood, a Figure quaint,
Tricked out in proud disguise of cast-off weeds
Which for that service had been husbanded,
By exhortation of my frugal Dame —
Motley accoutrement, of power to smile
At thorns, and brakes, and brambles, — and, in truth,
More raggèd than need was! O'er pathless rocks,
Through beds of matted fern, and tangled thickets,
Forcing my way, I came to one dear nook
Unvisited, where not a broken bough
Drooped with its withered leaves, ungracious sign
Of devastation; but the hazels rose
Tall and erect, with tempting clusters hung,
A virgin scene! — A little while I stood,
Breathing with such suppression of the heart

As joy delights in; and, with wise restraint
Voluptuous, fearless of a rival, eyed
The banquet; — or beneath the trees I sate
Among the flowers, and with the flowers I played;
A temper known to those, who, after long
And weary expectation, have been blest
With sudden happiness beyond all hope.
Perhaps it was a bower beneath whose leaves
The violets of five seasons re-appear
And fade, unseen by any human eye;
Where fairy water-breaks do murmur on
For ever; and I saw the sparkling foam,
And — with my cheek on one of those green stones
That, fleeced with moss, under the shady trees,
Lay round me, scattered like a flock of sheep —
I heard the murmur and the murmuring sound,
In that sweet mood when pleasure loves to pay
Tribute to ease; and, of its joy secure,
The heart luxuriates with indifferent things,
Wasting its kindliness on stocks and stones,
And on the vacant air. Then up I rose,
And dragged to earth both branch and bough, with crash
And merciless ravage: and the shady nook
Of hazels, and the green and mossy bower,
Deformed and sullied, patiently gave up
Their quiet being: and, unless I now
Confound my present feelings with the past;
Ere from the mutilated bower I turned
Exulting, rich beyond the wealth of kings,
I felt a sense of pain when I beheld
The silent trees, and saw the intruding sky —
Then, dearest Maiden, move along these shades
In gentleness of heart; with gentle hand
Touch — for there is a spirit in the woods.

"Strange fits of passion have I known"

Strange fits of passion have I known:
And I will dare to tell,
But in the Lover's ear alone,
What once to me befell.

When she I loved looked every day
Fresh as a rose in June,
I to her cottage bent my way,
Beneath an evening-moon.

Upon the moon I fixed my eye,
All over the wide lea;
With quickening pace my horse drew nigh
Those paths so dear to me.

And now we reached the orchard-plot;
And, as we climbed the hill,
The sinking moon to Lucy's cot
Came near, and nearer still.

In one of those sweet dreams I slept,
Kind Nature's gentlest boon!
And all the while my eyes I kept
On the descending moon.

My horse moved on; hoof after hoof
He raised, and never stopped:
When down behind the cottage roof,
At once, the bright moon dropped.

What fond and wayward thoughts will slide
Into a Lover's head!
"O mercy!" to myself I cried,
"If Lucy should be dead!"

"She dwelt among the untrodden ways"

She dwelt among the untrodden ways
    Beside the springs of Dove,
A Maid whom there were none to praise
    And very few to love:

A violet by a mossy stone
    Half hidden from the eye!
— Fair as a star, when only one
    Is shining in the sky.

She lived unknown, and few could know
  When Lucy ceased to be;
But she is in her grave, and, oh,
  The difference to me!

"I travelled among unknown men"

I travelled among unknown men,
  In lands beyond the sea;
Nor, England! did I know till then
  What love I bore to thee.

'Tis past, that melancholy dream!
  Nor will I quit thy shore
A second time; for still I seem
  To love thee more and more.

Among thy mountains did I feel
  The joy of my desire;
And she I cherished turned her wheel
  Beside an English fire.

Thy mornings showed, thy nights concealed
  The bowers where Lucy played;
And thine too is the last green field
  That Lucy's eyes surveyed.

"A slumber did my spirit seal"

A slumber did my spirit seal;
  I had no human fears:
She seemed a thing that could not feel
  The touch of earthly years.

No motion has she now, no force;
  She neither hears nor sees;
Rolled round in earth's diurnal course,
  With rocks, and stones, and trees.

Lucy Gray

OR, SOLITUDE

Oft I had heard of Lucy Gray:
And, when I crossed the wild,
I chanced to see at break of day
The solitary child.

No mate, no comrade Lucy knew;
She dwelt on a wide moor,
— The sweetest thing that ever grew
Beside a human door!

You yet may spy the fawn at play,
The hare upon the green;
But the sweet face of Lucy Gray
Will never more be seen.

"To-night will be a stormy night —
You to the town must go;
And take a lantern, Child, to light
Your mother through the snow."

"That, Father! will I gladly do:
'Tis scarcely afternoon —
The minster-clock has just struck two,
And yonder is the moon!"

At this the Father raised his hook,
And snapped a faggot-band;
He plied his work; — and Lucy took
The lantern in her hand.

Not blither is the mountain roe:
With many a wanton stroke
Her feet disperse the powdery snow,
That rises up like smoke.

The storm came on before its time:
She wandered up and down;
And many a hill did Lucy climb:
But never reached the town.

The wretched parents all that night
Went shouting far and wide;
But there was neither sound nor sight
To serve them for a guide.

At day-break on a hill they stood
That overlooked the moor;
And thence they saw the bridge of wood,
A furlong from their door.

They wept — and, turning homeward, cried,
"In heaven we all shall meet;"
— When in the snow the mother spied
The print of Lucy's feet.

Then downwards from the steep hill's edge
They tracked the footmarks small;
And through the broken hawthorn hedge,
And by the long stone-wall;

And then an open field they crossed:
The marks were still the same;
They tracked them on, nor ever lost;
And to the bridge they came.

They followed from the snowy bank
Those footmarks, one by one,
Into the middle of the plank;
And further there were none!

— Yet some maintain that to this day
She is a living child;
That you may see sweet Lucy Gray
Upon the lonesome wild.

O'er rough and smooth she trips along,
And never looks behind;
And sings a solitary song
That whistles in the wind.

"My heart leaps up when I behold"

My heart leaps up when I behold
    A rainbow in the sky:
So was it when my life began;
So is it now I am a man;
So be it when I shall grow old,
    Or let me die!
The Child is father of the Man;
And I could wish my days to be
Bound each to each by natural piety.

Resolution and Independence

I   There was a roaring in the wind all night;
    The rain came heavily and fell in floods;
    But now the sun is rising calm and bright;
    The birds are singing in the distant woods;
    Over his own sweet voice the Stock-dove broods;
    The Jay makes answer as the Magpie chatters;
    And all the air is filled with pleasant noise of waters.

II   All things that love the sun are out of doors;
    The sky rejoices in the morning's birth;
    The grass is bright with rain-drops; — on the moors
    The hare is running races in her mirth;
    And with her feet she from the plashy earth
    Raises a mist, that, glittering in the sun,
    Runs with her all the way, wherever she doth run.

III   I was a Traveller then upon the moor,
    I saw the hare that raced about with joy;
    I heard the woods and distant waters roar;
    Or heard them not, as happy as a boy:
    The pleasant season did my heart employ:
    My old remembrances went from me wholly;
    And all the ways of men, so vain and melancholy.

IV   But, as it sometimes chanceth, from the might
       Of joy in minds that can no further go,
       As high as we have mounted in delight
       In our dejection do we sink as low;
       To me that morning did it happen so;
       And fears and fancies thick upon me came;
       Dim sadness — and blind thoughts, I knew not, nor could name.

V   I heard the sky-lark warbling in the sky;
       And I bethought me of the playful hare:
       Even such a happy Child of earth am I;
       Even as these blissful creatures do I fare;
       Far from the world I walk, and from all care;
       But there may come another day to me —
       Solitude, pain of heart, distress, and poverty.

VI   My whole life I have lived in pleasant thought,
       As if life's business were a summer mood;
       As if all needful things would come unsought
       To genial faith, still rich in genial good;
       But how can He expect that others should
       Build for him, sow for him, and at his call
       Love him, who for himself will take no heed at all?

VII   I thought of Chatterton, the marvellous Boy,
       The sleepless Soul that perished in his pride;
       Of Him who walked in glory and in joy
       Following his plough, along the mountain-side:
       By our own spirits are we deified:
       We Poets in our youth begin in gladness;
       But thereof come in the end despondency and madness.

VIII   Now, whether it were by peculiar grace,
       A leading from above, a something given,
       Yet it befell, that, in this lonely place,
       When I with these untoward thoughts had striven,
       Beside a pool bare to the eye of heaven
       I saw a Man before me unawares:
       The oldest man he seemed that ever wore grey hairs.

IX   As a huge stone is sometimes seen to lie
       Couched on the bald top of an eminence;
       Wonder to all who do the same espy,
       By what means it could thither come, and whence;
       So that it seems a thing endued with sense:
       Like a sea-beast crawled forth, that on a shelf
       Of rock or sand reposeth, there to sun itself;

X   Such seemed this Man, not all alive nor dead,
       Nor all asleep — in his extreme old age:
       His body was bent double, feet and head
       Coming together in life's pilgrimage;
       As if some dire constraint of pain, or rage
       Of sickness felt by him in times long past,
       A more than human weight upon his frame had cast.

XI   Himself he propped, limbs, body, and pale face,
       Upon a long grey staff of shaven wood:
       And, still as I drew near with gentle pace,
       Upon the margin of that moorish flood
       Motionless as a cloud the old Man stood,
       That heareth not the loud winds when they call
       And moveth all together, if it move at all.

XII   At length, himself unsettling, he the pond
       Stirred with his staff, and fixedly did look
       Upon the muddy water, which he conned,
       As if he had been reading in a book:
       And now a stranger's privilege I took;
       And, drawing to his side, to him did say,
       "This morning gives us promise of a glorious day."

XIII   A gentle answer did the old Man make,
       In courteous speech which forth he slowly drew:
       And him with further words I thus bespake,
       "What occupation do you there pursue?
       This is a lonesome place for one like you."
       Ere he replied, a flash of mild surprise
       Broke from the sable orbs of his yet-vivid eyes,

XIV   His words came feebly, from a feeble chest,
But each in solemn order followed each,
With something of a lofty utterance drest —
Choice word and measured phrase, above the reach
Of ordinary men; a stately speech;
Such as grave Livers do in Scotland use,
Religious men, who give to God and man their dues.

XV   He told, that to these waters he had come
To gather leeches, being old and poor:
Employment hazardous and wearisome!
And he had many hardships to endure:
From pond to pond he roamed, from moor to moor;
Housing, with God's good help, by choice or chance,
And in this way he gained an honest maintenance.

XVI   The old Man still stood talking by my side;
But now his voice to me was like a stream
Scarce heard; nor word from word could I divide;
And the whole body of the Man did seem
Like one whom I had met with in a dream;
Or like a man from some far region sent,
To give me human strength, by apt admonishment.

XVII   My former thoughts returned: the fear that kills;
And hope that is unwilling to be fed;
Cold, pain, and labour, and all fleshly ills;
And mighty Poets in their misery dead.
— Perplexed, and longing to be comforted,
My question eagerly did I renew,
"How is it that you live, and what is it you do?"

XVIII   He with a smile did then his words repeat;
And said, that, gathering leeches, far and wide
He travelled; stirring thus above his feet
The waters of the pools where they abide.
"Once I could meet with them on every side;
But they have dwindled long by slow decay;
Yet still I persevere, and find them where I may."

XIX While he was talking thus, the lonely place,
      The old Man's shape, and speech — all troubled me:
      In my mind's eye I seemed to see him pace
      About the weary moors continually,
      Wandering about alone and silently.
      While I these thoughts within myself pursued,
      He, having made a pause, the same discourse renewed.

XX And soon with this he other matter blended,
      Cheerfully uttered, with demeanour kind,
      But stately in the main; and when he ended,
      I could have laughed myself to scorn to find
      In that decrepit Man so firm a mind.
      "God," said I, "be my help and stay secure;
      I'll think of the Leech-gatherer on the lonely moor!"

Composed upon Westminster Bridge, Sept. 3, 1802

Earth has not anything to show more fair:
Dull would he be of soul who could pass by
A sight so touching in its majesty:
This City now doth, like a garment, wear
The beauty of the morning; silent, bare,
Ships, towers, domes, theatres, and temples lie
Open unto the fields, and to the sky;
All bright and glittering in the smokeless air.
Never did sun more beautifully steep
In his first splendour, valley, rock, or hill;
Ne'er saw I, never felt, a calm so deep!
The river glideth at his own sweet will:
Dear God! the very houses seem asleep;
And all that mighty heart is lying still!

On the Extinction of the Venetian Republic

Once did She hold the gorgeous east in fee;
And was the safeguard of the west: the worth
Of Venice did not fall below her birth,
Venice, the eldest Child of Liberty.
She was a maiden City, bright and free;
No guile seduced, no force could violate;
And, when she took unto herself a Mate,
She must espouse the everlasting Sea.
And what if she had seen those glories fade,
Those titles vanish, and that strength decay;
Yet shall some tribute of regret be paid
When her long life hath reached its final day:
Men are we, and must grieve when even the Shade
Of that which once was great, is passed away.

To Toussaint L'Ouverture

Toussaint, the most unhappy man of men!
Whether the whistling Rustic tend his plough
Within thy hearing, or thy head be now
Pillowed in some deep dungeon's earless den; —
O miserable Chieftain! where and when
Wilt thou find patience? Yet die not; do thou
Wear rather in thy bonds a cheerful brow:
Though fallen thyself, never to rise again,
Live, and take comfort. Thou hast left behind
Powers that will work for thee; air, earth, and skies;
There's not a breathing of the common wind
That will forget thee; thou hast great allies;
Thy friends are exultations, agonies,
And love, and man's unconquerable mind.

In London, September 1802

O Friend! I know not which way I must look
For comfort, being, as I am, opprest,
To think that now our life is only drest
For show; mean handy-work of craftsman, cook,
Or groom! — We must run glittering like a brook
In the open sunshine, or we are unblest:
The wealthiest man among us is the best:
No grandeur now in nature or in book
Delights us. Rapine, avarice, expense,
This is idolatry; and these we adore:
Plain living and high thinking are no more:
The homely beauty of the good old cause
Is gone; our peace, our fearful innocence,
And pure religion breathing household laws.

London, 1802

Milton! thou should'st be living at this hour:
England hath need of thee: she is a fen
Of stagnant waters: altar, sword, and pen,
Fireside, the heroic wealth of hall and bower,
Have forfeited their ancient English dower
Of inward happiness. We are selfish men;
Oh! raise us up, return to us again;
And give us manners, virtue, freedom, power.
Thy soul was like a Star, and dwelt apart:
Thou hadst a voice whose sound was like the sea:
Pure as the naked heavens, majestic, free,
So didst thou travel on life's common way,
In cheerful godliness; and yet thy heart
The lowliest duties on herself did lay.

The Solitary Reaper

Behold her, single in the field,
Yon solitary Highland Lass!
Reaping and singing by herself;
Stop here, or gently pass!
Alone she cuts and binds the grain,
And sings a melancholy strain;
O listen! for the Vale profound
Is overflowing with the sound.

No Nightingale did ever chaunt
More welcome notes to weary bands
Of travellers in some shady haunt,
Among Arabian sands:
A voice so thrilling ne'er was heard
In spring-time from the Cuckoo-bird,
Breaking the silence of the seas
Among the farthest Hebrides.

Will no one tell me what she sings? —
Perhaps the plaintive numbers flow
For old, unhappy, far-off things,
And battles long ago:
Or is it some more humble lay,
Familiar matter of to-day?
Some natural sorrow, loss, or pain,
That has been, and may be again?

Whate'er the theme, the Maiden sang
As if her song could have no ending;
I saw her singing at her work,
And o'er the sickle bending; —
I listened, motionless and still;
And, as I mounted up the hill
The music in my heart I bore,
Long after it was heard no more.

"She was a Phantom of delight"

She was a Phantom of delight
When first she gleamed upon my sight;
A lovely Apparition, sent
To be a moment's ornament;
Her eyes as stars of Twilight fair;
Like Twilight's, too, her dusky hair;
But all things else about her drawn
From May-time and the cheerful Dawn;
A dancing Shape, an Image gay,
To haunt, to startle, and way-lay.

I saw her upon nearer view,
A Spirit, yet a Woman too!
Her household motions light and free,
And steps of virgin-liberty;
A countenance in which did meet
Sweet records, promises as sweet;
A Creature not too bright or good
For human nature's daily food;
For transient sorrows, simple wiles,
Praise, blame, love, kisses, tears, and smiles.

And now I see with eye serene
The very pulse of the machine;
A Being breathing thoughtful breath,
A Traveller between life and death;
The reason firm, the temperate will,
Endurance, foresight, strength, and skill;
A perfect Woman, nobly planned,
To warn, to comfort, and command;
And yet a Spirit still, and bright
With something of angelic light.

"I wandered lonely as a cloud"

I wandered lonely as a cloud
That floats on high o'er vales and hills,
When all at once I saw a crowd,
A host, of golden daffodils;

Beside the lake, beneath the trees,
Fluttering and dancing in the breeze.

Continuous as the stars that shine
And twinkle on the milky way,
They stretched in never-ending line
Along the margin of a bay:
Ten thousand saw I at a glance,
Tossing their heads in sprightly dance.

The waves beside them danced; but they
Out-did the sparkling waves in glee:
A poet could not but be gay,
In such a jocund company:
I gazed — and gazed — but little thought
What wealth the show to me had brought:

For oft, when on my couch I lie
In vacant or in pensive mood,
They flash upon that inward eye
Which is the bliss of solitude;
And then my heart with pleasure fills,
And dances with the daffodils.

Ode to Duty

Stern Daughter of the Voice of God!
O Duty! if that name thou love
Who art a light to guide, a rod
To check the erring, and reprove;
Thou, who art victory and law
When empty terrors overawe;
From vain temptations dost set free;
And calm'st the weary strife of frail humanity!

There are who ask not if thine eye
Be on them; who, in love and truth,
Where no misgiving is, rely
Upon the genial sense of youth:
Glad Hearts! without reproach or blot
Who do thy work, and know it not:

Oh! if through confidence misplaced
They fail, thy saving arms, dread Power! around them cast.

Serene will be our days and bright,
And happy will our nature be,
When love is an unerring light,
And joy its own security.
And they a blissful course may hold
Even now, who, not unwisely bold,
Live in the spirit of this creed;
Yet seek thy firm support, according to their need.

I, loving freedom, and untried;
No sport of every random gust,
Yet being to myself a guide,
Too blindly have reposed my trust:
And oft, when in my heart was heard
Thy timely mandate, I deferred
The task, in smoother walks to stray;
But thee I now would serve more strictly, if I may.

Through no disturbance of my soul,
Or strong compunction in me wrought,
I supplicate for thy control;
But in the quietness of thought:
Me this unchartered freedom tires;
I feel the weight of chance-desires:
My hopes no more must change their name,
I long for a repose that ever is the same.

Stern Lawgiver! yet thou dost wear
The Godhead's most benignant grace;
Nor know we anything so fair
As is the smile upon thy face:
Flowers laugh before thee on their beds
And fragrance in thy footing treads;
Thou dost preserve the stars from wrong;
And the most ancient heavens, through Thee, are fresh and strong.

To humbler functions, awful Power!
I call thee: I myself commend
Unto thy guidance from this hour;

Oh, let my weakness have an end!
Give unto me, made lowly wise,
The spirit of self-sacrifice;
The confidence of reason give;
And in the light of truth thy Bondman let me live!

"The Prelude": Book I, 340–400

Dust as we are, the immortal spirit grows
Like harmony in music; there is a dark
Inscrutable workmanship that reconciles
Discordant elements, makes them cling together
In one society. How strange, that all
The terrors, pains, and early miseries,
Regrets, vexations, lassitudes interfused
Within my mind, should e'er have borne a part,
And that a needful part, in making up
The calm existence that is mine when I
Am worthy of myself! Praise to the end!
Thanks to the means which Nature deigned to employ;
Whether her fearless visitings, or those
That came with soft alarm, like hurtless light
Opening the peaceful clouds; or she would use
Severer interventions, ministry
More palpable, as best might suit her aim.

One summer evening (led by her) I found
A little boat tied to a willow tree
Within a rocky cove, its usual home.
Straight I unloosed her chain, and stepping in
Pushed from the shore. It was an act of stealth
And troubled pleasure, nor without the voice
Of mountain-echoes did my boat move on;
Leaving behind her still, on either side,
Small circles glittering idly in the moon,
Until they melted all into one track
Of sparkling light. But now, like one who rows,
Proud of his skill, to reach a chosen point
With an unswerving line, I fixed my view
Upon the summit of a craggy ridge,

The horizon's utmost boundary; far above
Was nothing but the stars and the grey sky.
She was an elfin pinnace; lustily
I dipped my oars into the silent lake,
And, as I rose upon the stroke, my boat
Went heaving through the water like a swan;
When, from behind that craggy steep till then
The horizon's bound, a huge peak, black and huge,
As if with voluntary power instinct,
Upreared its head. I struck and struck again,
And growing still in stature the grim shape
Towered up between me and the stars, and still,
For so it seemed, with purpose of its own
And measured motion like a living thing,
Strode after me. With trembling oars I turned,
And through the silent water stole my way
Back to the covert of the willow tree;
There in her mooring-place I left my bark, —
And through the meadows homeward went, in grave
And serious mood; but after I had seen
That spectacle, for many days, my brain
Worked with a dim and undetermined sense
Of unknown modes of being; o'er my thoughts
There hung a darkness, call it solitude
Or blank desertion. No familiar shapes
Remained, no pleasant images of trees,
Of sea or sky, no colours of green fields;
But huge and mighty forms, that do not live
Like living men, moved slowly through the mind
By day, and were a trouble to my dreams.

"The Prelude": Book XI, 105–143

O pleasant exercise of hope and joy!
For mighty were the auxiliars which then stood
Upon our side, us who were strong in love!
Bliss was it in that dawn to be alive,
But to be young was very Heaven! O times,
In which the meagre, stale, forbidding ways
Of custom, law, and statute, took at once
The attraction of a country in romance!

When Reason seemed the most to assert her rights,
When most intent on making of herself
A prime enchantress — to assist the work,
Which then was going forward in her name!
Not favoured spots alone, but the whole Earth,
The beauty wore of promise — that which sets
(As at some moments might not be unfelt
Among the bowers of Paradise itself)
The budding rose above the rose full blown.
What temper at the prospect did not wake
To happiness unthought of? The inert
Were roused, and lively natures rapt away!
They who had fed their childhood upon dreams,
The play-fellows of fancy, who had made
All powers of swiftness, subtilty, and strength
Their ministers, — who in lordly wise had stirred
Among the grandest objects of the sense,
And dealt with whatsoever they found there
As if they had within some lurking right
To wield it; — they, too, who of gentle mood
Had watched all gentle motions, and to these
Had fitted their own thoughts, schemers more mild,
And in the region of their peaceful selves; —
Now was it that *both* found, the meek and lofty
Did both find, helpers to their hearts' desire,
And stuff at hand, plastic as they could wish, —
Were called upon to exercise their skill,
Not in Utopia, — subterranean fields, —
Or some secreted island, Heaven knows where!
But in the very world, which is the world
Of all of us, — the place where, in the end,
We find our happiness, or not at all!

Character of the Happy Warrior

Who is the happy Warrior? Who is he
That every man in arms should wish to be?
— It is the generous Spirit, who, when brought
Among the tasks of real life, hath wrought
Upon the plan that pleased his boyish thought:
Whose high endeavours are an inward light

That makes the path before him always bright:
Who, with a natural instinct to discern
What knowledge can perform, is diligent to learn;
Abides by this resolve, and stops not there,
But makes his moral being his prime care;
Who, doomed to go in company with Pain,
And Fear, and Bloodshed, miserable train!
Turns his necessity to glorious gain;
In face of these doth exercise a power
Which is our human nature's highest dower;
Controls them and subdues, transmutes, bereaves
Of their bad influence, and their good receives:
By objects, which might force the soul to abate
Her feeling, rendered more compassionate;
Is placable — because occasions rise
So often that demand such sacrifice;
More skilful in self-knowledge, even more pure,
As tempted more; more able to endure,
As more exposed to suffering and distress;
Thence, also, more alive to tenderness.
— 'Tis he whose law is reason; who depends
Upon that law as on the best of friends;
Whence, in a state where men are tempted still
To evil for a guard against worse ill,
And what in quality or act is best
Doth seldom on a right foundation rest,
He labours good on good to fix, and owes
To virtue every triumph that he knows:
— Who, if he rise to station of command,
Rises by open means; and there will stand
On honourable terms, or else retire,
And in himself possess his own desire;
Who comprehends his trust, and to the same
Keeps faithful with a singleness of aim;
And therefore does not stoop, nor lie in wait
For wealth, or honours, or for worldly state;
Whom they must follow; on whose head must fall,
Like showers of manna, if they come at all:
Whose powers shed round him in the common strife,
Or mild concerns of ordinary life,
A constant influence, a peculiar grace;
But who, if he be called upon to face

Some awful moment to which Heaven has joined
Great issues, good or bad for human kind,
Is happy as a Lover; and attired
With sudden brightness, like a Man inspired;
And, through the heat of conflict, keeps the law
In calmness made, and sees what he foresaw;
Or if an unexpected call succeed,
Come when it will, is equal to the need:
— He who, though thus endued as with a sense
And faculty for storm and turbulence,
Is yet a Soul whose master-bias leans
To homefelt pleasures and to gentle scenes;
Sweet images! which, wheresoe'er he be,
Are at his heart; and such fidelity
It is his darling passion to approve;
More brave for this, that he hath much to love: —
'Tis, finally, the Man, who, lifted high,
Conspicuous object in a Nation's eye,
Or left unthought-of in obscurity, —
Who, with a toward or untoward lot,
Prosperous or adverse, to his wish or not —
Plays, in the many games of life, that one
Where what he most doth value must be won:
Whom neither shape of danger can dismay,
Nor thought of tender happiness betray;
Who, not content that former worth stand fast,
Looks forward, persevering to the last,
From well to better, daily self-surpast:
Who, whether praise of him must walk the earth
For ever, and to noble deeds give birth,
Or he must fall, to sleep without his fame,
And leave a dead unprofitable name —
Finds comfort in himself and in his cause;
And, while the mortal mist is gathering, draws
His breath in confidence of Heaven's applause:
This is the happy Warrior; this is He
That every Man in arms should wish to be.

"The world is too much with us; late and soon"

The world is too much with us; late and soon,
Getting and spending, we lay waste our powers:
Little we see in Nature that is ours;
We have given our hearts away, a sordid boon!
The Sea that bares her bosom to the moon;
The winds that will be howling at all hours,
And are up-gathered now like sleeping flowers;
For this, for everything, we are out of tune;
It moves us not. — Great God! I'd rather be
A Pagan suckled in a creed outworn;
So might I, standing on this pleasant lea,
Have glimpses that would make me less forlorn;
Have sight of Proteus rising from the sea;
Or hear old Triton blow his wreathèd horn.

Ode:
Intimations of Immortality from
Recollections of Early Childhood

I

There was a time when meadow, grove, and stream,
The earth, and every common sight,
   To me did seem
  Apparelled in celestial light,
The glory and the freshness of a dream.
It is not now as it hath been of yore; —
  Turn wheresoe'er I may,
   By night or day,
The things which I have seen I now can see no more.

II

   The Rainbow comes and goes,
   And lovely is the Rose,
   The Moon doth with delight
Look round her when the heavens are bare,
    Waters on a starry night
    Are beautiful and fair;
   The sunshine is a glorious birth;
   But yet I know, where'er I go,
That there hath past away a glory from the earth.

III

Now, while the birds thus sing a joyous song,
   And while the young lambs bound
    As to the tabor's sound,
To me alone there came a thought of grief:
A timely utterance gave that thought relief,
    And I again am strong:
The cataracts blow their trumpets from the steep;
No more shall grief of mine the season wrong;
I hear the Echoes through the mountains throng,
The Winds come to me from the fields of sleep,
    And all the earth is gay;
     Land and sea
   Give themselves up to jollity,
    And with the heart of May
   Doth every Beast keep holiday; —
    Thou Child of Joy,
Shout round me, let me hear thy shouts, thou happy
    Shepherd-boy!

IV

Ye blessèd Creatures, I have heard the call
   Ye to each other make; I see
The heavens laugh with you in your jubilee;
    My heart is at your festival,
    My head hath its coronal,
The fulness of your bliss, I feel — I feel it all.
    Oh evil day! if I were sullen
    While Earth herself is adorning,

This sweet May-morning,
And the Children are culling
On every side,
In a thousand valleys far and wide,
Fresh flowers; while the sun shines warm,
And the Babe leaps up on his Mother's arm: —
I hear, I hear, with joy I hear!
— But there's a Tree, of many, one,
A single Field which I have looked upon,
Both of them speak of something that is gone:
The Pansy at my feet
Doth the same tale repeat:
Whither is fled the visionary gleam?
Where is it now, the glory and the dream?

V

Our birth is but a sleep and a forgetting:
The Soul that rises with us, our life's Star,
Hath had elsewhere its setting,
And cometh from afar:
Not in entire forgetfulness,
And not in utter nakedness,
But trailing clouds of glory do we come
From God, who is our home:
Heaven lies about us in our infancy!
Shades of the prison-house begin to close
Upon the growing Boy,
But He beholds the light, and whence it flows,
He sees it in his joy;
The Youth, who daily farther from the east
Must travel, still is Nature's Priest,
And by the vision splendid

Is on his way attended;
At length the Man perceives it die away,
And fade into the light of common day.

VI

Earth fills her lap with pleasures of her own;
Yearnings she hath in her own natural kind,

And, even with something of a Mother's mind,
    And no unworthy aim,
    The homely Nurse doth all she can
To make her Foster-child, her Inmate Man,
    Forget the glories he hath known,
And that imperial palace whence he came.

VII

Behold the Child among his new-born blisses,
A six years' Darling of a pigmy size!
See, where 'mid work of his own hand he lies,
Fretted by sallies of his mother's kisses,
With light upon him from his father's eyes!
See, at his feet, some little plan or chart,
Some fragment from his dream of human life,
Shaped by himself with newly-learned art;
    A wedding or a festival,
    A mourning or a funeral;
     And this hath now his heart,
    And unto this he frames his song:
      Then will he fit his tongue
To dialogues of business, love, or strife;
    But it will not be long
    Ere this be thrown aside,
    And with new joy and pride
The little Actor cons another part;
Filling from time to time his "humorous stage"
With all the Persons, down to palsied Age,
That Life brings with her in her equipage;
    As if his whole vocation
    Were endless imitation.

VIII

Thou, whose exterior semblance doth belie
    Thy Soul's immensity;
Thou best Philosopher, who yet dost keep
Thy heritage, thou Eye among the blind,
That, deaf and silent, read'st the eternal deep,
Haunted for ever by the eternal mind, —
    Mighty Prophet! Seer blest!
    On whom those truths do rest,

Which we are toiling all our lives to find,
In darkness lost, the darkness of the grave;
Thou, over whom thy Immortality
Broods like the Day, a Master o'er a Slave,
A Presence which is not to be put by;
Thou little Child, yet glorious in the might
Of heaven-born freedom on thy being's height,
Why with such earnest pains dost thou provoke
The years to bring the inevitable yoke,
Thus blindly with thy blessedness at strife?
Full soon thy Soul shall have her earthly freight,
And custom lie upon thee with a weight,
Heavy as frost, and deep almost as life!

IX

O joy! that in our embers
Is something that doth live,
That nature yet remembers
What was so fugitive!
The thought of our past years in me doth breed
Perpetual benediction: not indeed
For that which is most worthy to be blest —
Delight and liberty, the simple creed
Of Childhood, whether busy or at rest,
With new-fledged hope still fluttering in his breast: —
Not for these I raise
The song of thanks and praise;
But for those obstinate questionings
Of sense and outward things,
Fallings from us, vanishings;
Blank misgivings of a Creature
Moving about in worlds not realised,
High instincts before which our mortal Nature
Did tremble like a guilty Thing surprised:
But for those first affections,
Those shadowy recollections,
Which, be they what they may,
Are yet the fountain light of all our day,
Are yet a master light of all our seeing;
Uphold us, cherish, and have power to make
Our noisy years seem moments in the being

Of the eternal Silence: truths that wake,
　　To perish never;
Which neither listlessness, nor mad endeavour,
　　Nor Man nor Boy,
Nor all that is at enmity with joy,
Can utterly abolish or destroy!
　　Hence in a season of calm weather
　　Though inland far we be,
Our Souls have sight of that immortal sea
　　Which brought us hither,
　　Can in a moment travel thither,
And see the Children sport upon the shore,
And hear the mighty waters rolling evermore.

X

Then sing, ye Birds, sing, sing a joyous song!
　　And let the young Lambs bound
　　As to the tabor's sound!
We in thought will join your throng,
　　Ye that pipe and ye that play,
　　Ye that through your hearts to-day
　　Feel the gladness of the May!
What though the radiance which was once so bright
Be now for ever taken from my sight,
　　Though nothing can bring back the hour
Of splendour in the grass, of glory in the flower;
　　We will grieve not, rather find
　　Strength in what remains behind;
　　In the primal sympathy
　　Which having been must ever be;
　　In the soothing thoughts that spring
　　Out of human suffering;
　　In the faith that looks through death,
In years that bring the philosophic mind.

XI

And O, ye Fountains, Meadows, Hills, and Groves,
Forebode not any severing of our loves!

Yet in my heart of hearts I feel your might;
I only have relinquished one delight
To live beneath your more habitual sway.
I love the Brooks which down their channels fret,
Even more than when I tripped lightly as they;
The innocent brightness of a new-born Day
                    Is lovely yet;
The Clouds that gather round the setting sun
Do take a sober colouring from an eye
That hath kept watch o'er man's mortality;
Another race hath been, and other palms are won.
Thanks to the human heart by which we live,
Thanks to its tenderness, its joys, and fears,
To me the meanest flower that blows can give
Thoughts that do often lie too deep for tears.

Mutability

From low to high doth dissolution climb,
And sink from high to low, along a scale
Of awful notes, whose concord shall not fail;
A musical but melancholy chime,
Which they can hear who meddle not with crime,
Nor avarice, nor over-anxious care.
Truth fails not; but her outward forms that bear
The longest date do melt like frosty rime,
That in the morning whitened hill and plain
And is no more; drop like the tower sublime
Of yesterday, which royally did wear
His crown of weeds, but could not even sustain
Some casual shout that broke the silent air,
Or the unimaginable touch of Time.

"Scorn not the Sonnet"

Scorn not the Sonnet; Critic, you have frowned,
Mindless of its just honours; with this key
Shakspeare unlocked his heart; the melody
Of this small lute gave ease to Petrarch's wound;
A thousand times this pipe did Tasso sound;
With it Camöens soothed an exile's grief;
The Sonnet glittered a gay myrtle leaf
Amid the cypress with which Dante crowned
His visionary brow: a glow-worm lamp,
It cheered mild Spenser, called from Faery-land
To struggle through dark ways; and, when a damp
Fell round the path of Milton, in his hand
The Thing became a trumpet; whence he blew
Soul-animating strains — alas, too few!

Extempore Effusion upon the Death of James Hogg

When first, descending from the moor-lands,
I saw the Stream of Yarrow glide
Along a bare and open valley,
The Ettrick Shepherd was my guide.

When last along its banks I wandered,
Through groves that had begun to shed
Their golden leaves upon the pathways,
My steps the Border-minstrel led.

The mighty Minstrel breathes no longer,
'Mid mouldering ruins low he lies;
And death upon the braes of Yarrow,
Has closed the Shepherd-poet's eyes:

Nor has the rolling year twice measured,
From sign to sign, its stedfast course,
Since every mortal power of Coleridge
Was frozen at its marvellous source;

The rapt One, of the godlike forehead,
The heaven-eyed creature sleeps in earth:
And Lamb, the frolic and the gentle,
Has vanished from his lonely hearth.

Like clouds that rake the mountain-summits,
Or waves that own no curbing hand,
How fast has brother followed brother
From sunshine to the sunless land!

Yet I, whose lids from infant slumber
Were earlier raised, remain to hear
A timid voice, that asks in whispers,
"Who next will drop and disappear?"

Our haughty life is crowned with darkness,
Like London with its own black wreath,
On which with thee, O Crabbe! forth-looking,
I gazed from Hampstead's breezy heath.

As if but yesterday departed,
Thou too art gone before; but why,
O'er ripe fruit, seasonably gathered,
Should frail survivors heave a sigh?

Mourn rather for that holy Spirit,
Sweet as the spring, as ocean deep;
For Her who, ere her summer faded,
Has sunk into a breathless sleep.

No more of old romantic sorrows,
For slaughtered Youth or love-lorn Maid!
With sharper grief is Yarrow smitten,
And Ettrick mourns with her their Poet dead.

SAMUEL TAYLOR COLERIDGE (1772–1834)

This Lime-Tree Bower My Prison

Well, they are gone, and here must I remain,
This lime-tree bower my prison! I have lost
Beauties and feelings, such as would have been
Most sweet to my remembrance even when age
Had dimm'd mine eyes to blindness! They, meanwhile,
Friends, whom I never more may meet again,
On springy heath, along the hill-top edge,
Wander in gladness, and wind down, perchance,
To that still roaring dell, of which I told;
The roaring dell, o'erwooded, narrow, deep,
And only speckled by the mid-day sun;
Where its slim trunk the ash from rock to rock
Flings arching like a bridge; — that branchless ash,
Unsunn'd and damp, whose few poor yellow leaves
Ne'er tremble in the gale, yet tremble still,
Fann'd by the water-fall! and there my friends
Behold the dark green file of long lank weeds,
That all at once (a most fantastic sight!)
Still nod and drip beneath the dripping edge
Of the blue clay-stone.

                Now, my friends emerge
Beneath the wide wide Heaven — and view again
The many-steepled tract magnificent
Of hilly fields and meadows, and the sea,
With some fair bark, perhaps, whose sails light up
The slip of smooth clear blue betwixt two Isles
Of purple shadow! Yes! they wander on
In gladness all; but thou, methinks, most glad,
My gentle-hearted Charles! for thou hast pined
And hunger'd after Nature, many a year,

In the great City pent, winning thy way
With sad yet patient soul, through evil and pain
And strange calamity! Ah! slowly sink
Behind the western ridge, thou glorious Sun!
Shine in the slant beams of the sinking orb,
Ye purple heath-flowers! richlier burn, ye clouds!
Live in the yellow light, ye distant groves!
And kindle, thou blue Ocean! So my friend
Struck with deep joy may stand, as I have stood,
Silent with swimming sense; yea, gazing round
On the wide landscape, gaze till all doth seem
Less gross than bodily; and of such hues
As veil the Almighty Spirit, when yet he makes
Spirits perceive his presence.

              A delight
Comes sudden on my heart, and I am glad
As I myself were there! Nor in this bower,
This little lime-tree bower, have I not mark'd
Much that has sooth'd me. Pale beneath the blaze
Hung the transparent foliage; and I watch'd
Some broad and sunny leaf, and lov'd to see
The shadow of the leaf and stem above
Dappling its sunshine! And that walnut-tree
Was richly ting'd, and a deep radiance lay
Full on the ancient ivy, which usurps
Those fronting elms, and now, with blackest mass
Makes their dark branches gleam a lighter hue
Through the late twilight: and though now the bat
Wheels silent by, and not a swallow twitters,
Yet still the solitary humble-bee
Sings in the bean-flower! Henceforth I shall know
That Nature ne'er deserts the wise and pure;
No plot so narrow, be but Nature there,
No waste so vacant, but may well employ
Each faculty of sense, and keep the heart
Awake to Love and Beauty! and sometimes
'Tis well to be bereft of promis'd good,
That we may lift the soul, and contemplate
With lively joy the joys we cannot share.
My gentle-hearted Charles! when the last rook
Beat its straight path along the dusky air

Homewards, I blest it! deeming its black wing
(Now a dim speck, now vanishing in light)
Had cross'd the mighty Orb's dilated glory,
While thou stood'st gazing; or, when all was still,
Flew creeking o'er thy head, and had a charm
For thee, my gentle-hearted Charles, to whom
No sound is dissonant which tells of Life.

The Dungeon

And this place our forefathers made for man!
This is the process of our love and wisdom,
To each poor brother who offends against us —
Most innocent, perhaps — and what if guilty?
Is this the only cure? Merciful God!
Each pore and natural outlet shrivell'd up
By Ignorance and parching Poverty,
His energies roll back upon his heart,
And stagnate and corrupt; till chang'd to poison,
They break out on him, like a loathsome plague-spot;
Then we call in our pamper'd mountebanks —
And this is their best cure! uncomforted
And friendless solitude, groaning and tears,
And savage faces, at the clanking hour,
Seen through the steams and vapour of his dungeon,
By the lamp's dismal twilight! So he lies
Circled with evil, till his very soul
Unmoulds its essence, hopelessly deform'd
By sights of ever more deformity!

With other ministrations thou, O Nature!
Healest thy wandering and distemper'd child:
Thou pourest on him thy soft influences,
Thy sunny hues, fair forms, and breathing sweets,
Thy melodies of woods, and winds, and waters,
Till he relent, and can no more endure
To be a jarring and a dissonant thing,
Amid this general dance and minstrelsy;
But, bursting into tears, wins back his way,
His angry spirit heal'd and harmoniz'd
By the benignant touch of Love and Beauty.

The Rime of the Ancient Mariner

IN SEVEN PARTS

Facile credo, plures esse Naturas invisibiles quam visibiles in rerum universitate. Sed horum omnium familiam quis nobis enarrabit? et gradus et cognationes et discrimina et singulorum munera? Quid agunt? quae loca habitant? Harum rerum notitiam semper ambivit ingenium humanum, nunquam attigit. Juvat, interea, non diffiteor, quandoque in animo, tanquam in tabula, majoris et melioris mundi imaginem contemplari: ne mens assuefacta hodiernae vitae minutiis se contrahat nimis, et tota subsidat in pusillas cogitationes. Sed veritati interea invigilandum est, modusque servandus, ut certa ab incertis, diem a nocte, distinguamus. — T BURNET, *Archaeol. Phil.* p. 68.*

ARGUMENT

How a Ship having passed the Line was driven by storms to the cold Country towards the South Pole; and how from thence she made her course to the tropical Latitude of the Great Pacific Ocean; and of the strange things that befell; and in what manner the Ancyent Marinere came back to his own Country.

PART I

An ancient Mariner meeteth three Gallants bidden to a wedding-feast, and detaineth one.

It is an ancient Mariner,
And he stoppeth one of three.
'By thy long grey beard and glittering eye,
Now wherefore stopp'st thou me?

The Bridegroom's doors are opened wide,
And I am next of kin;
The guests are met, the feast is set:
May'st hear the merry din.'

---

*TRANSLATION: I readily believe that in the totality of things there are more invisible than visible natures. But who shall recount to us the family of all these things? and their degrees and relationships and distinctive signs and their individual functions? What do they do? What places do they inhabit? The human mind has always solicited knowledge of these matters but has never attained it. Meanwhile, I do not deny, it is sometimes pleasant to contemplate the image of a greater and better world in the mind as if in a picture, lest the mind, accustomed to the trivia of modern life, should shrink excessively and sink completely into petty musings. But at the same time one must be intent upon truth, and moderation must be observed, so that we may distinguish the sure from the unsure, day from night.

He holds him with his skinny hand,
'There was a ship,' quoth he.
'Hold off! unhand me, grey-beard loon!'
Eftsoons his hand dropt he.

The Wedding-
Guest is
spellbound by the
eye of the old
seafaring man,
and constrained to
hear his tale.

He holds him with his glittering eye —
The Wedding-Guest stood still,
And listens like a three years' child:
The Mariner hath his will.

The Wedding-Guest sat on a stone:
He cannot choose but hear;
And thus spake on that ancient man,
The bright-eyed Mariner.

'The ship was cheered, the harbour cleared,
Merrily did we drop
Below the kirk, below the hill,
Below the lighthouse top.

The Mariner tells
how the ship sailed
southward with a
good wind and fair
weather, till it
reached the line.

The Sun came up upon the left,
Out of the sea came he!
And he shone bright, and on the right
Went down into the sea.

Higher and higher every day,
Till over the mast at noon —'
The Wedding-Guest here beat his breast,
For he heard the loud bassoon.

The Wedding-
Guest heareth the
bridal music; but
the Mariner
continueth his tale.

The bride hath paced into the hall,
Red as a rose is she;
Nodding their heads before her goes
The merry minstrelsy.

The Wedding-Guest he beat his breast,
Yet he cannot choose but hear;
And thus spake on that ancient man,
The bright-eyed Mariner.

The ship driven by
a storm toward
the south pole.

'And now the STORM-BLAST came, and he
Was tyrannous and strong:
He struck with his o'ertaking wings,
And chased us south along.

With sloping masts and dipping prow,
As who pursued with yell and blow
Still treads the shadow of his foe,
And forward bends his head,
The ship drove fast, loud roared the blast,
And southward aye we fled.

And now there came both mist and snow,
And it grew wondrous cold:
And ice, mast-high, came floating by,
As green as emerald.

The land of ice, and of fearful sounds where no living thing was to be seen.

And through the drifts the snowy clifts
Did send a dismal sheen:
Nor shapes of men nor beasts we ken —
The ice was all between.

The ice was here, the ice was there,
The ice was all around:
It cracked and growled, and roared and howled,
Like noises in a swound!

Till a great sea-bird, called the Albatross, came through the snow-fog, and was received with great joy and hospitality.

At length did cross an Albatross,
Thorough the fog it came;
As if it had been a Christian soul,
We hailed it in God's name.

It ate the food it ne'er had eat,
And round and round it flew.
The ice did split with a thunder-fit;
The helmsman steered us through!

And lo! the Albatross proveth a bird of good omen, and followeth the ship as it returned northward through fog and floating ice.

And a good south wind sprung up behind;
The Albatross did follow,
And every day, for food or play,
Came to the mariner's hollo!

In mist or cloud, on mast or shroud,
It perched for vespers nine;
Whiles all the night, through fog-smoke white,
Glimmered the white Moon-shine.'

The ancient Mariner inhospitably killeth the pious bird of good omen.

'God save thee, ancient Mariner!
From the fiends, that plague thee thus! —
Why look'st thou so?' — With my cross-bow
I shot the ALBATROSS.

PART II

The Sun now rose upon the right:
Out of the sea came he,
Still hid in mist, and on the left
Went down into the sea.

And the good south wind still blew behind,
But no sweet bird did follow,
Nor any day for food or play
Came to the mariners' hollo!

*His shipmates cry
out against the
ancient Mariner,
for killing the bird
of good luck.*

And I had done a hellish thing,
And it would work 'em woe:
For all averred, I had killed the bird
That made the breeze to blow.
Ah wretch! said they, the bird to slay,
That made the breeze to blow!

*But when the fog
cleared off, they
justify the same,
and thus make
themselves
accomplices in the
crime.*

Nor dim nor red, like God's own head,
The glorious Sun uprist:
Then all averred, I had killed the bird
That brought the fog and mist.
'Twas right, said they, such birds to slay,
That bring the fog and mist.

*The fair breeze
continues; the ship
enters the Pacific
Ocean, and sails
northward, even
till it reaches the
Line.*

The fair breeze blew, the white foam flew,
The furrow followed free;
We were the first that ever burst
Into that silent sea.

*The ship hath been
suddenly
becalmed.*

Down dropt the breeze, the sails dropt down,
'Twas sad as sad could be;
And we did speak only to break
The silence of the sea!

All in a hot and copper sky,
The bloody Sun, at noon,
Right up above the mast did stand,
No bigger than the Moon.

Day after day, day after day,
We stuck, nor breath nor motion;
As idle as a painted ship
Upon a painted ocean.

And the Albatross begins to be avenged.

Water, water, every where,
And all the boards did shrink;
Water, water, every where,
Nor any drop to drink.

The very deep did rot: O Christ!
That ever this should be!
Yea, slimy things did crawl with legs
Upon the slimy sea.

About, about, in reel and rout
The death-fires danced at night;
The water, like a witch's oils,
Burnt green, and blue and white.

A Spirit had followed them; one of the invisible inhabitants of this planet, neither departed souls nor angels; concerning whom the learned Jew, Josephus, and the Platonic Constantinopolitan, Michael Psellus, may be consulted. They are very numerous, and there is no climate or element without one or more.

And some in dreams assuréd were
Of the Spirit that plagued us so;
Nine fathom deep he had followed us
From the land of mist and snow.

And every tongue, through utter drought,
Was withered at the root;
We could not speak, no more than if
We had been choked with soot.

The shipmates, in their sore distress, would fain throw the whole guilt on the ancient Mariner: in sign whereof they hang the dead sea-bird round his neck.

Ah! well a-day! what evil looks
Had I from old and young!
Instead of the cross, the Albatross
About my neck was hung.

PART III

There passed a weary time. Each throat
Was parched, and glazed each eye.
A weary time! a weary time!
How glazed each weary eye,

*The ancient
Mariner beholdeth
a sign in the
element afar off.*

When looking westward, I beheld
A something in the sky.

At first it seemed a little speck,
And then it seemed a mist;
It moved and moved, and took at last
A certain shape, I wist.

A speck, a mist, a shape, I wist!
And still it neared and neared:
As if it dodged a water-sprite,
It plunged and tacked and veered.

*At its nearer
approach, it
seemeth him to be
a ship; and at a
dear ransom he
freeth his speech
from the bonds of
thirst.*

A flash of joy;

With throats unslaked, with black lips baked,
We could nor laugh nor wail;
Through utter drought all dumb we stood!
I bit my arm, I sucked the blood,
And cried, A sail! a sail!

With throats unslaked, with black lips baked,
Agape they heard me call:
Gramercy! they for joy did grin,
And all at once their breath drew in,
As they were drinking all.

*And horror follows.
For can it be a ship
that comes onward
without wind or
tide?*

See! see! (I cried) she tacks no more!
Hither to work us weal;
Without a breeze, without a tide,
She steadies with upright keel!

The western wave was all a-flame.
The day was well nigh done!
Almost upon the western wave
Rested the broad bright Sun;
When that strange shape drove suddenly
Betwixt us and the Sun.

*It seemeth him but
the skeleton of a
ship.*

And straight the Sun was flecked with bars,
(Heaven's Mother send us grace!)
As if through a dungeon-grate he peered
With broad and burning face.

*And its ribs are
seen as bars on the
face of the setting
Sun.*

Alas! (thought I, and my heart beat loud)
How fast she nears and nears!
Are those *her* sails that glance in the Sun,
Like restless gossameres?

The Spectre-Woman and her Deathmate, and no other on board the skeleton ship.

Are those *her* ribs through which the Sun
Did peer, as through a grate?
And is that Woman all her crew?
Is that a DEATH? and are there two?
Is DEATH that woman's mate?

Like vessel, like crew!

Her lips were red, *her* looks were free,
Her locks were yellow as gold:
Her skin was as white as leprosy,
The Night-mare LIFE-IN-DEATH was she,
Who thicks man's blood with cold.

Death and Life-in-Death have diced for the ship's crew, and she (the latter) winneth the ancient Mariner.

The naked hulk alongside came,
And the twain were casting dice;
'The game is done! I've won! I've won!'
Quoth she, and whistles thrice.

No twilight within the courts of the Sun.

The Sun's rim dips; the stars rush out:
At one stride comes the dark;
With far-heard whisper, o'er the sea,
Off shot the spectre-bark.

At the rising of the Moon,

We listened and looked sideways up!
Fear at my heart, as at a cup,
My life-blood seemed to sip!
The stars were dim, and thick the night,
The steersman's face by his lamp gleamed white;
From the sails the dew did drip —
Till clomb above the eastern bar
The hornéd Moon, with one bright star
Within the nether tip.

One after another,

One after one, by the star-dogged Moon,
Too quick for groan or sigh,
Each turned his face with a ghastly pang,
And cursed me with his eye.

His shipmates drop down dead.

Four times fifty living men,
(And I heard nor sigh nor groan)
With heavy thump, a lifeless lump,
They dropped down one by one.

But Life-in-Death begins her work on the ancient Mariner.

The souls did from their bodies fly, —
They fled to bliss or woe!
And every soul, it passed me by,
Like the whizz of my cross-bow!

PART IV

*The Wedding-
Guest feareth that
a Spirit is talking
to him;*

'I fear thee, ancient Mariner!
I fear thy skinny hand!
And thou art long, and lank, and brown,
As is the ribbed sea-sand.

I fear thee and thy glittering eye,
And thy skinny hand, so brown.' —

*But the ancient
Mariner assureth
him of his bodily
life, and
proceedeth to relate
his horrible
penance.*

Fear not, fear not, thou Wedding-Guest!
This body dropt not down.

Alone, alone, all, all alone,
Alone on a wide wide sea!
And never a saint took pity on
My soul in agony.

*He despiseth the
creatures of the
calm,*

The many men, so beautiful!
And they all dead did lie:
And a thousand thousand slimy things
Lived on; and so did I.

*And envieth that
they should live,
and so many lie
dead.*

I looked upon the rotting sea,
And drew my eyes away;
I looked upon the rotting deck,
And there the dead men lay.

I looked to heaven, and tried to pray;
But or ever a prayer had gusht,
A wicked whisper came, and made
My heart as dry as dust.

I closed my lids, and kept them close,
And the balls like pulses beat;
For the sky and the sea, and the sea and the sky
Lay like a load on my weary eye,
And the dead were at my feet.

*But the curse liveth
for him in the eye
of the dead men.*

The cold sweat melted from their limbs,
Nor rot nor reek did they:
The look with which they looked on me
Had never passed away.

An orphan's curse would drag to hell
A spirit from on high;
But oh! more horrible than that

Is the curse in a dead man's eye!
Seven days, seven nights, I saw that curse,
And yet I could not die.

*In his loneliness
and fixedness he
yearneth towards
the journeying
Moon, and the
stars that still
sojourn, yet still
move onward; and
every where the
blue sky belongs to
them, and is their
appointed rest, and*

The moving Moon went up the sky,
And no where did abide:
Softly she was going up,
And a star or two beside —

Her beams bemocked the sultry main,
Like April hoar-frost spread;
But where the ship's huge shadow lay,
The charmèd water burnt alway
A still and awful red.

*their native country and their own natural homes, which they enter unannounced, as
lords that are certainly expected and yet there is a silent joy at their arrival.*

*By the light of the
Moon he beholdeth
God's creatures of
the great calm.*

Beyond the shadow of the ship,
I watched the water-snakes:
They moved in tracks of shining white,
And when they reared, the elfish light
Fell off in hoary flakes.

Within the shadow of the ship
I watched their rich attire:
Blue, glossy green, and velvet black,
They coiled and swam; and every track
Was a flash of golden fire.

*Their beauty and
their happiness.*

*He blesseth them
in his heart.*

O happy living things! no tongue
Their beauty might declare:
A spring of love gushed from my heart,
And I blessed them unaware:
Sure my kind saint took pity on me,
And I blessed them unaware.

*The spell begins to
break.*

The self-same moment I could pray;
And from my neck so free
The Albatross fell off, and sank
Like lead into the sea.

PART V

Oh sleep! it is a gentle thing,
Beloved from pole to pole!

To Mary Queen the praise be given!
She sent the gentle sleep from Heaven,
That slid into my soul.

By grace of the
holy Mother, the
ancient Mariner is
refreshed with rain.

The silly buckets on the deck,
That had so long remained,
I dreamt that they were filled with dew;
And when I awoke, it rained.

My lips were wet, my throat was cold,
My garments all were dank;
Sure I had drunken in my dreams,
And still my body drank.

I moved, and could not feel my limbs:
I was so light — almost
I thought that I had died in sleep,
And was a blessèd ghost.

He heareth sounds
and seeth strange
sights and
commotions in the
sky and the
element.

And soon I heard a roaring wind:
It did not come anear;
But with its sound it shook the sails,
That were so thin and sere.

The upper air burst into life!
And a hundred fire-flags sheen,
To and fro they were hurried about!
And to and fro, and in and out,
The wan stars danced between.

And the coming wind did roar more loud,
And the sails did sigh like sedge;
And the rain poured down from one black cloud;
The Moon was at its edge.

The thick black cloud was cleft, and still
The Moon was at its side:
Like waters shot from some high crag,
The lightning fell with never a jag,
A river steep and wide.

The bodies of the
ship's crew are
inspired and the
ship moves on;

The loud wind never reached the ship,
Yet now the ship moved on!
Beneath the lightning and the Moon
The dead men gave a groan.

They groaned, they stirred, they all uprose,
Nor spake, nor moved their eyes;
It had been strange, even in a dream,
To have seen those dead men rise.

The helmsman steered, the ship moved on;
Yet never a breeze up-blew;
The mariners all 'gan work the ropes,
Where they were wont to do;
They raised their limbs like lifeless tools —
We were a ghastly crew.

The body of my brother's son
Stood by me, knee to knee:
The body and I pulled at one rope,
But he said nought to me.

But not by the souls of the men, nor by dæmons of earth or middle air, but by a blessed troop of angelic spirits, sent down by the invocation of the guardian saint.

'I fear thee, ancient Mariner!'
Be calm, thou Wedding-Guest!
'Twas not those souls that fled in pain,
Which to their corses came again,
But a troop of spirits blest:

For when it dawned — they dropped their arms,
And clustered round the mast;
Sweet sounds rose slowly through their mouths,
And from their bodies passed.

Around, around, flew each sweet sound,
Then darted to the Sun;
Slowly the sounds came back again,
Now mixed, now one by one.

Sometimes a-dropping from the sky
I heard the sky-lark sing;
Sometimes all little birds that are,
How they seemed to fill the sea and air
With their sweet jargoning!

And now 'twas like all instruments,
Now like a lonely flute;
And now it is an angel's song,
That makes the heavens be mute.

It ceased; yet still the sails made on
A pleasant noise till noon,
A noise like of a hidden brook
In the leafy month of June,
That to the sleeping woods all night
Singeth a quiet tune.

Till noon we quietly sailed on,
Yet never a breeze did breathe:
Slowly and smoothly went the ship,
Moved onward from beneath.

*The lonesome
Spirit from the
south-pole carries
on the ship as far
as the Line, in
obedience to the
angelic troop, but
still requireth
vengeance.*

Under the keel nine fathom deep,
From the land of mist and snow,
The spirit slid: and it was he
That made the ship to go.
The sails at noon left off their tune,
And the ship stood still also.

The Sun, right up above the mast,
Had fixed her to the ocean:
But in a minute she 'gan stir,
With a short uneasy motion —
Backwards and forwards half her length
With a short uneasy motion.

Then like a pawing horse let go,
She made a sudden bound:
It flung the blood into my head,
And I fell down in a swound.

*The Polar Spirit's
fellow-dæmons, the
invisible
inhabitants of the
element, take part
in his wrong; and
two of them relate,
one to the other,
that penance long
and heavy for the
ancient Mariner
hath been accorded
to the Polar Spirit,
who returneth
southward.*

How long in that same fit I lay,
I have not to declare;
But ere my living life returned,
I heard and in my soul discerned
Two voices in the air.

'Is it he?' quoth one, 'Is this the man?
By him who died on cross,
With his cruel bow he laid full low
The harmless Albatross.

The spirit who bideth by himself
In the land of mist and snow,
He loved the bird that loved the man
Who shot him with his bow.'

The other was a softer voice,
As soft as honey-dew:
Quoth he, 'The man hath penance done,
And penance more will do.'

PART VI

FIRST VOICE

'But tell me, tell me! speak again,
Thy soft response renewing —
What makes that ship drive on so fast?
What is the ocean doing?'

SECOND VOICE

'Still as a slave before his lord,
The ocean hath no blast;
His great bright eye most silently
Up to the Moon is cast —

If he may know which way to go;
For she guides him smooth or grim.
See, brother, see! how graciously
She looketh down on him.'

FIRST VOICE

The Mariner hath been cast into a trance; for the angelic power causeth the vessel to drive northward faster than human life could endure.

'But why drives on that ship so fast,
Without or wave or wind?'

SECOND VOICE

'The air is cut away before,
And closes from behind.

Fly, brother, fly! more high, more high!
Or we shall be belated:
For slow and slow that ship will go,
When the Mariner's trance is abated.'

The supernatural motion is retarded; the Mariner awakes, and his penance begins anew.

I woke, and we were sailing on
As in a gentle weather:
'Twas night, calm night, the moon was high;
The dead men stood together.

All stood together on the deck,
For a charnel-dungeon fitter:
All fixed on me their stony eyes,
That in the Moon did glitter.

The pang, the curse, with which they died,
Had never passed away:
I could not draw my eyes from theirs,
Nor turn them up to pray.

The curse is finally
expiated.

And now this spell was snapt: once more
I viewed the ocean green,
And looked far forth, yet little saw
Of what had else been seen —

Like one, that on a lonesome road
Doth walk in fear and dread,
And having once turned round walks on,
And turns no more his head;
Because he knows, a frightful fiend
Doth close behind him tread.

But soon there breathed a wind on me,
Nor sound nor motion made:
Its path was not upon the sea,
In ripple or in shade.

It raised my hair, it fanned my cheek
Like a meadow-gale of spring —
It mingled strangely with my fears,
Yet it felt like a welcoming.

Swiftly, swiftly flew the ship,
Yet she sailed softly too:
Sweetly, sweetly blew the breeze —
On me alone it blew.

And the ancient
Mariner beholdeth
his native country.

Oh! dream of joy! is this indeed
The light-house top I see?
Is this the hill? is this the kirk?
Is this mine own countree?

We drifted o'er the harbour-bar,
And I with sobs did pray —

O let me be awake, my God!
Or let me sleep alway.

The harbour-bay was clear as glass,
So smoothly it was strewn!
And on the bay the moonlight lay,
And the shadow of the Moon.

The rock shone bright, the kirk no less,
That stands above the rock:
The moonlight steeped in silentness
The steady weathercock.

*The angelic spirits
leave the dead
bodies,*

And the bay was white with silent light,
Till rising from the same,
Full many shapes, that shadows were,
In crimson colours came.

*And appear in
their own forms of
light.*

A little distance from the prow
Those crimson shadows were:
I turned my eyes upon the deck —
Oh, Christ! what saw I there!

Each corse lay flat, lifeless and flat,
And, by the holy rood!
A man all light, a seraph-man,
On every corse there stood.

This seraph-band, each waved his hand:
It was a heavenly sight!
They stood as signals to the land,
Each one a lovely light;

This seraph-band, each waved his hand,
No voice did they impart —
No voice; but oh! the silence sank
Like music on my heart.

But soon I heard the dash of oars,
I heard the Pilot's cheer;
My head was turned perforce away
And I saw a boat appear.

The Pilot and the Pilot's boy,
I heard them coming fast:

Dear Lord in Heaven! it was a joy
The dead men could not blast.

I saw a third — I heard his voice:
It is the Hermit good!
He singeth loud his godly hymns
That he makes in the wood.
He'll shrieve my soul, he'll wash away
The Albatross's blood.

PART VII

The Hermit of the
Wood,

This Hermit good lives in that wood
Which slopes down to the sea.
How loudly his sweet voice he rears!
He loves to talk with marineres
That come from a far countree.

He kneels at morn, and noon, and eve —
He hath a cushion plump:
It is the moss that wholly hides
The rotted old oak-stump.

The skiff-boat neared: I heard them talk,
'Why, this is strange, I trow!
Where are those lights so many and fair,
That signal made but now?'

Approacheth the
ship with wonder.

'Strange, by my faith!' the Hermit said —
'And they answered not our cheer!
The planks looked warped! and see those sails,
How thin they are and sere!
I never saw aught like to them,
Unless perchance it were

Brown skeletons of leaves that lag
My forest-brook along;
When the ivy-tod is heavy with snow,
And the owlet whoops to the wolf below,
That eats the she-wolf's young.'

'Dear Lord! it hath a fiendish look —
(The Pilot made reply)
I am a-feared' — 'Push on, push on!'
Said the Hermit cheerily.

The boat came closer to the ship,
But I nor spake nor stirred;
The boat came close beneath the ship,
And straight a sound was heard.

The ship suddenly sinketh.

Under the water it rumbled on,
Still louder and more dread:
It reached the ship, it split the bay;
The ship went down like lead.

The ancient Mariner is saved in the Pilot's boat.

Stunned by that loud and dreadful sound,
Which sky and ocean smote,
Like one that hath been seven days drowned
My body lay afloat;
But swift as dreams, myself I found
Within the Pilot's boat.

Upon the whirl, where sank the ship,
The boat spun round and round;
And all was still, save that the hill
Was telling of the sound.

I moved my lips — the Pilot shrieked
And fell down in a fit;
The holy Hermit raised his eyes,
And prayed where he did sit.

I took the oars: the Pilot's boy,
Who now doth crazy go,
Laughed loud and long, and all the while
His eyes went to and fro.
'Ha! ha!' quoth he, 'full plain I see,
The Devil knows how to row.'

And now, all in my own countree,
I stood on the firm land!
The Hermit stepped forth from the boat,
And scarcely he could stand.

The ancient Mariner earnestly entreateth the Hermit to shrieve him; and the penance of life falls on him.

'O shrieve me, shrieve me, holy man!'
The Hermit crossed his brow.
'Say quick,' quoth he, 'I bid thee say —
What manner of man art thou?'

Forthwith this frame of mine was wrenched
With a woful agony,

Which forced me to begin my tale;
And then it left me free.

*And ever and anon
throughout his
future life an
agony constraineth
him to travel from
land to land;*

Since then, at an uncertain hour,
That agony returns:
And till my ghastly tale is told,
This heart within me burns.

I pass, like night, from land to land;
I have strange power of speech;
That moment that his face I see,
I know the man that must hear me:
To him my tale I teach.

What loud uproar bursts from that door!
The wedding-guests are there:
But in the garden-bower the bride
And bride-maids singing are:
And hark the little vesper bell,
Which biddeth me to prayer!

O Wedding-Guest! this soul hath been
Alone on a wide wide sea:
So lonely 'twas, that God himself
Scarce seeméd there to be.

O sweeter than the marriage-feast,
'Tis sweeter far to me,
To walk together to the kirk
With a goodly company! —

To walk together to the kirk,
And all together pray,
While each to his great Father bends,
Old men, and babes, and loving friends
And youths and maidens gay!

*And to teach, by
his own example,
love and reverence
to all things that
God made and
loveth.*

Farewell, farewell! but this I tell
To thee, thou Wedding-Guest!
He prayeth well, who loveth well
Both man and bird and beast.

He prayeth best, who loveth best
All things both great and small;
For the dear God who loveth us,
He made and loveth all.

The Mariner, whose eye is bright,
Whose beard with age is hoar,
Is gone: and now the Wedding-Guest
Turned from the bridegroom's door.

He went like one that hath been stunned,
And is of sense forlorn:
A sadder and a wiser man,
He rose the morrow morn.

On a Ruined House in a Romantic Country

And this reft house is that the which he built,
Lamented Jack! And here his malt he pil'd,
Cautious in vain! These rats that squeak so wild,
Squeak, not unconscious of their father's guilt.
Did ye not see her gleaming thro' the glade?
Belike, 'twas she, the maiden all forlorn.
What though she milk no cow with crumpled horn,
Yet *aye* she haunts the dale where *erst* she stray'd;
And *aye* beside her stalks her amorous knight!
Still on his thighs their wonted brogues are worn,
And thro' those brogues, still tatter'd and betorn,
His hindward charms gleam an unearthly white;
As when thro' broken clouds at night's high noon
Peeps in fair fragments forth the full-orb'd harvest-moon!

Christabel

PART I

'Tis the middle of night by the castle clock,
And the owls have awakened the crowing cock;
Tu — whit! — Tu — whoo!
And hark, again! the crowing cock,
How drowsily it crew.

Sir Leoline, the Baron rich,
Hath a toothless mastiff bitch;
From her kennel beneath the rock
She maketh answer to the clock,
Four for the quarters, and twelve for the hour;
Ever and aye, by shine and shower,
Sixteen short howls, not over loud;
Some say, she sees my lady's shroud.

Is the night chilly and dark?
The night is chilly, but not dark,
The thin gray cloud is spread on high,
It covers but not hides the sky.
The moon is behind, and at the full;
And yet she looks both small and dull.
The night is chill, the cloud is gray:
'Tis a month before the month of May,
And the Spring comes slowly up this way.

The lovely lady, Christabel,
Whom her father loves so well,
What makes her in the wood so late,
A furlong from the castle gate?
She had dreams all yesternight
Of her own betrothéd knight;
And she in the midnight wood will pray
For the weal of her lover that's far away.

She stole along, she nothing spoke,
The sighs she heaved were soft and low,
And naught was green upon the oak

But moss and rarest misletoe:
She kneels beneath the huge oak tree,
And in silence prayeth she.

The lady sprang up suddenly,
The lovely lady, Christabel!
It moaned as near, as near can be,
But what it is she cannot tell. —
On the other side it seems to be,
Of the huge, broad-breasted, old oak tree.

The night is chill; the forest bare;
Is it the wind that moaneth bleak?
There is not wind enough in the air
To move away the ringlet curl
From the lovely lady's cheek —
There is not wind enough to twirl
The one red leaf, the last of its clan,
That dances as often as dance it can,
Hanging so light, and hanging so high,
On the topmost twig that looks up at the sky.

Hush, beating heart of Christabel!
Jesu, Maria, shield her well!
She folded her arms beneath her cloak,
And stole to the other side of the oak.
        What sees she there?

There she sees a damsel bright,
Drest in a silken robe of white,
That shadowy in the moonlight shone:
The neck that made that white robe wan,
Her stately neck, and arms were bare;
Her blue-veined feet unsandal'd were,
And wildly glittered here and there
The gems entangled in her hair.

I guess, 'twas frightful there to see
A lady so richly clad as she —
Beautiful exceedingly!

Mary mother, save me now!
(Said Christabel,) And who art thou?

The lady strange made answer meet,
And her voice was faint and sweet: —
Have pity on my sore distress,
I scarce can speak for weariness:
Stretch forth thy hand, and have no fear!
Said Christabel, How camest thou here?
And the lady, whose voice was faint and sweet,
Did thus pursue her answer meet: —

My sire is of a noble line,
And my name is Geraldine:
Five warriors seized me yestermorn,
Me, even me, a maid forlorn:
They choked my cries with force and fright,
And tied me on a palfrey white.
The palfrey was as fleet as wind,
And they rode furiously behind.
They spurred amain, their steeds were white:
And once we crossed the shade of night.
As sure as Heaven shall rescue me,
I have no thought what men they be;
Nor do I know how long it is
(For I have lain entranced I wis)
Since one, the tallest of the five,
Took me from the palfrey's back,
A weary woman, scarce alive.
Some muttered words his comrades spoke:
He placed me underneath this oak;
He swore they would return with haste;
Whither they went I cannot tell —
I thought I heard, some minutes past,
Sounds as of a castle bell.
Stretch forth thy hand (thus ended she),
And help a wretched maid to flee.

Then Christabel stretched forth her hand,
And comforted fair Geraldine:
O well, bright dame! may you command
The service of Sir Leoline;
And gladly our stout chivalry
Will he send forth and friends withal

To guide and guard you safe and free
Home to your noble father's hall.

She rose: and forth with steps they passed
That strove to be, and were not, fast.
Her gracious stars the lady blest,
And thus spake on sweet Christabel:
All our household are at rest,
The hall as silent as the cell;
Sir Leoline is weak in health,
And may not well awakened be,
But we will move as if in stealth,
And I beseech your courtesy,
This night, to share your couch with me.

They crossed the moat, and Christabel
Took the key that fitted well;
A little door she opened straight,
All in the middle of the gate;
The gate that was ironed within and without,
Where an army in battle array had marched out.
The lady sank, belike through pain,
And Christabel with might and main
Lifted her up, a weary weight,
Over the threshold of the gate:
Then the lady rose again,
And moved, as she were not in pain.

So free from danger, free from fear,
They crossed the court: right glad they were.
And Christabel devoutly cried
To the lady by her side,
Praise we the Virgin all divine
Who hath rescued thee from thy distress!
Alas, alas! said Geraldine,
I cannot speak for weariness.
So free from danger, free from fear,
They crossed the court: right glad they were.

Outside her kennel, the mastiff old
Lay fast asleep, in moonshine cold.
The mastiff old did not awake,
Yet she an angry moan did make!

And what can ail the mastiff bitch?
Never till now she uttered yell
Beneath the eye of Christabel.
Perhaps it is the owlet's scritch:
For what can ail the mastiff bitch?

They passed the hall, that echoes still,
Pass as lightly as you will!
The brands were flat, the brands were dying,
Amid their own white ashes lying;
But when the lady passed, there came
A tongue of light, a fit of flame;
And Christabel saw the lady's eye,
And nothing else saw she thereby,
Save the boss of the shield of Sir Leoline tall,
Which hung in a murky old niche in the wall.
O softly tread, said Christabel,
My father seldom sleepeth well.

Sweet Christabel her feet doth bare,
And jealous of the listening air
They steal their way from stair to stair,
Now in glimmer, and now in gloom,
And now they pass the Baron's room,
As still as death, with stifled breath!
And now have reached her chamber door;
And now doth Geraldine press down
The rushes of the chamber floor.

The moon shines dim in the open air,
And not a moonbeam enters here.
But they without its light can see
The chamber carved so curiously,
Carved with figures strange and sweet,
All made out of the carver's brain,
For a lady's chamber meet:
The lamp with twofold silver chain
Is fastened to an angel's feet.

The silver lamp burns dead and dim;
But Christabel the lamp will trim.
She trimmed the lamp, and made it bright,
And left it swinging to and fro,

While Geraldine, in wretched plight,
Sank down upon the floor below.

O weary lady, Geraldine,
I pray you, drink this cordial wine!
It is a wine of virtuous powers;
My mother made it of wild flowers.

And will your mother pity me,
Who am a maiden most forlorn?
Christabel answered — Woe is me!
She died the hour that I was born.
I have heard the grey-haired friar tell
How on her death-bed she did say,
That she should hear the castle-bell
Strike twelve upon my wedding-day.
O mother dear! that thou wert here!
I would, said Geraldine, she were!
But soon with altered voice, said she —
'Off, wandering mother! Peak and pine!
I have power to bid thee flee.'
Alas! what ails poor Geraldine?
Why stares she with unsettled eye?
Can she the bodiless dead espy?
And why with hollow voice cries she,
'Off, woman, off! this hour is mine —
Though thou her guardian spirit be,
Off, woman, off! 'tis given to me.'

Then Christabel knelt by the lady's side,
And raised to heaven her eyes so blue —
Alas! said she, this ghastly ride —
Dear lady! it hath wildered you!
The lady wiped her moist cold brow,
And faintly said, ' 'tis over now!'

Again the wild-flower wine she drank:
Her fair large eyes 'gan glitter bright,
And from the floor whereon she sank,
The lofty lady stood upright:
She was most beautiful to see,
Like a lady of a far countrée.

And thus the lofty lady spake —
'All they who live in the upper sky,
Do love you, holy Christabel!
And you love them, and for their sake
And for the good which me befel,
Even I in my degree will try,
Fair maiden, to requite you well.
But now unrobe yourself; for I
Must pray, ere yet in bed I lie.'

Quoth Christabel, So let it be!
And as the lady bade, did she.
Her gentle limbs did she undress,
And lay down in her loveliness.

But through her brain of weal and woe
So many thoughts moved to and fro,
That vain it were her lids to close;
So half-way from the bed she rose,
And on her elbow did recline
To look at the lady Geraldine.

Beneath the lamp the lady bowed,
And slowly rolled her eyes around;
Then drawing in her breath aloud,
Like one that shuddered, she unbound
The cincture from beneath her breast:
Her silken robe, and inner vest,
Dropt to her feet, and full in view,
Behold! her bosom and half her side —
A sight to dream of, not to tell!
O shield her! shield sweet Christabel!

Yet Geraldine nor speaks nor stirs;
Ah! what a stricken look was hers!
Deep from within she seems half-way
To lift some weight with sick assay,
And eyes the maid and seeks delay;
Then suddenly, as one defied,
Collects herself in scorn and pride,
And lay down by the Maiden's side! —
And in her arms the maid she took,
                    Ah wel-a-day!

And with low voice and doleful look
These words did say:
'In the touch of this bosom there worketh a spell,
Which is lord of thy utterance, Christabel!
Thou knowest to-night, and wilt know to-morrow,
This mark of my shame, this seal of my sorrow;
       But vainly thou warrest,
         For this is alone in
       Thy power to declare,
         That in the dim forest
        Thou heard'st a low moaning,
And found'st a bright lady, surpassingly fair;
And didst bring her home with thee in love and in charity,
To shield her and shelter her from the damp air.'

THE CONCLUSION TO PART I

It was a lovely sight to see
The lady Christabel, when she
Was praying at the old oak tree.
       Amid the jaggéd shadows
       Of mossy leafless boughs,
       Kneeling in the moonlight,
       To make her gentle vows;
Her slender palms together prest,
Heaving sometimes on her breast;
Her face resigned to bliss or bale —
Her face, oh call it fair not pale,
And both blue eyes more bright than clear,
Each about to have a tear.

With open eyes (ah woe is me!)
Asleep, and dreaming fearfully,
Fearfully dreaming, yet, I wis,
Dreaming that alone, which is —
O sorrow and shame! Can this be she,
The lady, who knelt at the old oak tree?
And lo! the worker of these harms,
That holds the maiden in her arms,
Seems to slumber still and mild,
As a mother with her child.

A star hath set, a star hath risen,
O Geraldine! since arms of thine
Have been the lovely lady's prison.
O Geraldine! one hour was thine —
Thou'st had thy will! By tairn and rill,
The night-birds all that hour were still.
But now they are jubilant anew,
From cliff and tower, tu — whoo! tu — whoo!
Tu — whoo! tu — whoo! from wood and fell!

And see! the lady Christabel
Gathers herself from out her trance;
Her limbs relax, her countenance
Grows sad and soft; the smooth thin lids
Close o'er her eyes; and tears she sheds —
Large tears that leave the lashes bright!
And oft the while she seems to smile
As infants at a sudden light!

Yea, she doth smile, and she doth weep,
Like a youthful hermitess,
Beauteous in a wilderness,
Who, praying always, prays in sleep.
And, if she move unquietly,
Perchance, 'tis but the blood so free
Comes back and tingles in her feet.
No doubt, she hath a vision sweet.
What if her guardian spirit 'twere,
What if she knew her mother near?
But this she knows, in joys and woes,
That saints will aid if men will call:
For the blue sky bends over all!

PART II

Each matin bell, the Baron saith,
Knells us back to a world of death.
These words Sir Leoline first said,
When he rose and found his lady dead:
These words Sir Leoline will say
Many a morn to his dying day!

And hence the custom and law began
That still at dawn the sacristan,
Who duly pulls the heavy bell,
Five and forty beads must tell
Between each stroke — a warning knell,
Which not a soul can choose but hear
From Bratha Head to Wyndermere.

Saith Bracy the bard, So let it knell!
And let the drowsy sacristan
Still count as slowly as he can!
There is no lack of such, I ween,
As well fill up the space between.
In Langdale Pike and Witch's Lair,
And Dungeon-ghyll so foully rent,
With ropes of rock and bells of air
Three sinful sextons' ghosts are pent,
Who all give back, one after t'other,
The death-note to their living brother;
And oft too, by the knell offended,
Just as their one! two! three! is ended,
The devil mocks the doleful tale
With a merry peal from Borodale.

The air is still! through mist and cloud
That merry peal comes ringing loud;
And Geraldine shakes off her dread,
And rises lightly from the bed;
Puts on her silken vestments white,
And tricks her hair in lovely plight,
And nothing doubting of her spell
Awakens the lady Christabel.
'Sleep you, sweet lady Christabel?
I trust that you have rested well.'

And Christabel awoke and spied
The same who lay down by her side —
O rather say, the same whom she
Raised up beneath the old oak tree!
Nay, fairer yet! and yet more fair!
For she belike hath drunken deep
Of all the blessedness of sleep!

And while she spake, her looks, her air
Such gentle thankfulness declare,
That (so it seemed) her girded vests
Grew tight beneath her heaving breasts.
'Sure I have sinn'd!' said Christabel,
'Now heaven be praised if all be well!'
And in low faltering tones, yet sweet,
Did she the lofty lady greet
With such perplexity of mind
As dreams too lively leave behind.

So quickly she rose, and quickly arrayed
Her maiden limbs, and having prayed
That He, who on the cross did groan,
Might wash away her sins unknown,
She forthwith led fair Geraldine
To meet her sire, Sir Leoline.

The lovely maid and the lady tall
Are pacing both into the hall,
And pacing on through page and groom,
Enter the Baron's presence-room.

The Baron rose, and while he prest
His gentle daughter to his breast,
With cheerful wonder in his eyes
The lady Geraldine espies,
And gave such welcome to the same,
As might beseem so bright a dame!

But when he heard the lady's tale,
And when she told her father's name,
Why waxed Sir Leoline so pale,
Murmuring o'er the name again,
Lord Roland de Vaux of Tryermaine?

Alas! they had been friends in youth;
But whispering tongues can poison truth;
And constancy lives in realms above;
And life is thorny; and youth is vain;
And to be wroth with one we love
Doth work like madness in the brain.
And thus it chanced, as I divine,

With Roland and Sir Leoline.
Each spake words of high disdain
And insult to his heart's best brother:
They parted — ne'er to meet again!
But never either found another
To free the hollow heart from paining —
They stood aloof, the scars remaining,
Like cliffs which had been rent asunder;
A dreary sea now flows between; —
But neither heat, nor frost, nor thunder,
Shall wholly do away, I ween,
The marks of that which once hath been.

Sir Leoline, a moment's space,
Stood gazing on the damsel's face:
And the youthful Lord of Tryermaine
Came back upon his heart again.

O then the Baron forgot his age,
His noble heart swelled high with rage;
He swore by the wounds in Jesu's side
He would proclaim it far and wide,
With trump and solemn heraldry,
That they, who thus had wronged the dame,
Were base as spotted infamy!
'And if they dare deny the same,
My herald shall appoint a week,
And let the recreant traitors seek
My tourney court — that there and then
I may dislodge their reptile souls
From the bodies and forms of men!'
He spake: his eye in lightning rolls!
For the lady was ruthlessly seized; and he kenned
In the beautiful lady the child of his friend!

And now the tears were on his face,
And fondly in his arms he took
Fair Geraldine, who met the embrace,
Prolonging it with joyous look.
Which when she viewed, a vision fell
Upon the soul of Christabel,
The vision of fear, the touch and pain!

She shrunk and shuddered, and saw again —
(Ah, woe is me! Was it for thee,
Thou gentle maid! such sights to see?)

Again she saw that bosom old,
Again she felt that bosom cold,
And drew in her breath with a hissing sound:
Whereat the Knight turned wildly round,
And nothing saw, but his own sweet maid
With eyes upraised, as one that prayed.

The touch, the sight, had passed away,
And in its stead that vision blest,
Which comforted her after-rest
While in the lady's arms she lay,
Had put a rapture in her breast,
And on her lips and o'er her eyes
Spread smiles like light!
                                          With new surprise,
'What ails then my belovéd child?'
The Baron said — His daughter mild
Made answer, 'All will yet be well!'
I ween, she had no power to tell
Aught else: so mighty was the spell.

Yet he, who saw this Geraldine,
Had deemed her sure a thing divine:
Such sorrow with such grace she blended,
As if she feared she had offended
Sweet Christabel, that gentle maid!
And with such lowly tones she prayed
She might be sent without delay
Home to her father's mansion.
                                          'Nay!
Nay, by my soul!' said Leoline.
'Ho! Bracy the bard, the charge be thine!
Go thou, with music sweet and loud,
And take two steeds with trappings proud,
And take the youth whom thou lov'st best
To bear thy harp, and learn thy song,
And clothe you both in solemn vest,
And over the mountains haste along,

Lest wandering folk, that are abroad,
Detain you on the valley road.

'And when he has crossed the Irthing flood,
My merry bard! he hastes, he hastes
Up Knorren Moor, through Halegarth Wood,
And reaches soon that castle good
Which stands and threatens Scotland's wastes.

'Bard Bracy! bard Bracy! your horses are fleet,
Ye must ride up the hall, your music so sweet,
More loud than your horses' echoing feet!
And loud and loud to Lord Roland call,
Thy daughter is safe in Langdale hall!
Thy beautiful daughter is safe and free —
Sir Leoline greets thee thus through me!
He bids thee come without delay
With all thy numerous array
And take thy lovely daughter home:
And he will meet thee on the way
With all his numerous array
White with their panting palfreys' foam:
And, by mine honour! I will say,
That I repent me of the day
When I spake words of fierce disdain
To Roland de Vaux of Tryermaine! —
— For since that evil hour hath flown,
Many a summer's sun hath shone;
Yet ne'er found I a friend again
Like Roland de Vaux of Tryermaine.'

The lady fell, and clasped his knees,
Her face upraised, her eyes o'erflowing;
And Bracy replied, with faltering voice,
His gracious Hail on all bestowing! —
'Thy words, thou sire of Christabel,
Are sweeter than my harp can tell;
Yet might I gain a boon of thee,
This day my journey should not be,
So strange a dream hath come to me,
That I had vowed with music loud
To clear yon wood from thing unblest,

Warned by a vision in my rest!
For in my sleep I saw that dove,
That gentle bird, whom thou dost love,
And call'st by thy own daughter's name —
Sir Leoline! I saw the same
Fluttering, and uttering fearful moan,
Among the green herbs in the forest alone.
Which when I saw and when I heard,
I wonder'd what might ail the bird;
For nothing near it could I see,
Save the grass and green herbs underneath the old tree.

'And in my dream methought I went
To search out what might there be found;
And what the sweet bird's trouble meant,
That thus lay fluttering on the ground.
I went and peered, and could descry
No cause for her distressful cry;
But yet for her dear lady's sake
I stooped, methought, the dove to take,
When lo! I saw a bright green snake
Coiled around its wings and neck.
Green as the herbs on which it couched,
Close by the dove's its head it crouched;
And with the dove it heaves and stirs,
Swelling its neck as she swelled hers!
I woke; it was the midnight hour,
The clock was echoing in the tower;
But though my slumber was gone by,
This dream it would not pass away —
It seems to live upon my eye!
And thence I vowed this self-same day
With music strong and saintly song
To wander through the forest bare,
Lest aught unholy loiter there.'

Thus Bracy said: the Baron, the while,
Half-listening heard him with a smile;
Then turned to Lady Geraldine,
His eyes made up of wonder and love;
And said in courtly accents fine,
'Sweet maid, Lord Roland's beauteous dove,

With arms more strong than harp or song,
Thy sire and I will crush the snake!'
He kissed her forehead as he spake,
And Geraldine in maiden wise
Casting down her large bright eyes,
With blushing cheek and courtesy fine
She turned her from Sir Leoline;
Softly gathering up her train,
That o'er her right arm fell again;
And folded her arms across her chest,
And couched her head upon her breast,
And looked askance at Christabel ——
Jesu, Maria, shield her well!

A snake's small eye blinks dull and shy;
And the lady's eyes they shrunk in her head,
Each shrunk up to a serpent's eye,
And with somewhat of malice, and more of dread,
At Christabel she looked askance! —
One moment — and the sight was fled!
But Christabel in dizzy trance
Stumbling on the unsteady ground
Shuddered aloud, with a hissing sound;
And Geraldine again turned round,
And like a thing, that sought relief,
Full of wonder and full of grief,
She rolled her large bright eyes divine
Wildly on Sir Leoline.

The maid, alas! her thoughts are gone,
She nothing sees — no sight but one!
The maid, devoid of guile and sin,
I know not how, in fearful wise,
So deeply had she drunken in
That look, those shrunken serpent eyes,
That all her features were resigned
To this sole image in her mind:
And passively did imitate
That look of dull and treacherous hate!
And thus she stood, in dizzy trance,
Still picturing that look askance
With forced unconscious sympathy

Full before her father's view ——
As far as such a look could be
In eyes so innocent and blue!

And when the trance was o'er, the maid
Paused awhile, and inly prayed:
Then falling at the Baron's feet,
'By my mother's soul do I entreat
That thou this woman send away!'
She said: and more she could not say:
For what she knew she could not tell,
O'er-mastered by the mighty spell.

Why is thy cheek so wan and wild,
Sir Leoline? Thy only child
Lies at thy feet, thy joy, thy pride,
So fair, so innocent, so mild;
The same, for whom thy lady died!
O by the pangs of her dear mother
Think thou no evil of thy child!
For her, and thee, and for no other,
She prayed the moment ere she died:
Prayed that the babe for whom she died,
Might prove her dear lord's joy and pride!
    That prayer her deadly pangs beguiled,
            Sir Leoline!
    And wouldst thou wrong thy only child,
            Her child and thine?

Within the Baron's heart and brain
If thoughts, like these, had any share,
They only swelled his rage and pain,
And did but work confusion there.
His heart was cleft with pain and rage,
His cheeks they quivered, his eyes were wild,
Dishonoured thus in his old age;
Dishonoured by his only child,
And all his hospitality
To the wronged daughter of his friend
By more than woman's jealousy
Brought thus to a disgraceful end —
He rolled his eye with stern regard

Upon the gentle minstrel bard,
And said in tones abrupt, austere —
'Why, Bracy! dost thou loiter here?
I bade thee hence!' The bard obeyed;
And turning from his own sweet maid,
The agéd knight, Sir Leoline,
Led forth the lady Geraldine!

THE CONCLUSION TO PART II

A little child, a limber elf,
Singing, dancing to itself,
A fairy thing with red round cheeks,
That always finds, and never seeks,
Makes such a vision to the sight
As fills a father's eyes with light;
And pleasures flow in so thick and fast
Upon his heart, that he at last
Must needs express his love's excess
With words of unmeant bitterness.
Perhaps 'tis pretty to force together
Thoughts so all unlike each other;
To mutter and mock a broken charm,
To dally with wrong that does no harm.
Perhaps 'tis tender too and pretty
At each wild word to feel within
A sweet recoil of love and pity.
And what, if in a world of sin
(O sorrow and shame should this be true!)
Such giddiness of heart and brain
Comes seldom save from rage and pain,
So talks as it's most used to do.

Frost at Midnight

The Frost performs its secret ministry,
Unhelped by any wind. The owlet's cry
Came loud — and hark, again! loud as before.
The inmates of my cottage, all at rest,
Have left me to that solitude, which suits
Abstruser musings: save that at my side
My cradled infant slumbers peacefully.
'Tis calm indeed! so calm, that it disturbs
And vexes meditation with its strange
And extreme silentness. Sea, hill, and wood,
This populous village! Sea, and hill, and wood,
With all the numberless goings-on of life,
Inaudible as dreams! the thin blue flame
Lies on my low-burnt fire, and quivers not;
Only that film, which fluttered on the grate,
Still flutters there, the sole unquiet thing.
Methinks, its motion in this hush of nature
Gives it dim sympathies with me who live,
Making it a companionable form,
Whose puny flaps and freaks the idling Spirit
By its own moods interprets, every where
Echo or mirror seeking of itself,
And makes a toy of Thought.

                          But O! how oft,
How oft, at school, with most believing mind,
Presageful, have I gazed upon the bars,
To watch that fluttering *stranger*! and as oft
With unclosed lids, already had I dreamt
Of my sweet birth-place, and the old church-tower,
Whose bells, the poor man's only music, rang
From morn to evening, all the hot Fair-day,
So sweetly, that they stirred and haunted me
With a wild pleasure, falling on mine ear
Most like articulate sounds of things to come!
So gazed I, till the soothing things, I dreamt,
Lulled me to sleep, and sleep prolonged my dreams!

And so I brooded all the following morn,
Awed by the stern preceptor's face, mine eye
Fixed with mock study on my swimming book:
Save if the door half opened, and I snatched
A hasty glance, and still my heart leaped up,
For still I hoped to see the *stranger's* face,
Townsman, or aunt, or sister more beloved,
My play-mate when we both were clothed alike!

Dear Babe, that sleepest cradled by my side,
Whose gentle breathings, heard in this deep calm,
Fill up the interspersèd vacancies
And momentary pauses of the thought!
My babe so beautiful! it thrills my heart
With tender gladness, thus to look at thee,
And think that thou shalt learn far other lore,
And in far other scenes! For I was reared
In the great city, pent 'mid cloisters dim,
And saw nought lovely but the sky and stars.
But *thou*, my babe! shalt wander like a breeze
By lakes and sandy shores, beneath the crags
Of ancient mountain, and beneath the clouds,
Which image in their bulk both lakes and shores
And mountain crags: so shalt thou see and hear
The lovely shapes and sounds intelligible
Of that eternal language, which thy God
Utters, who from eternity doth teach
Himself in all, and all things in himself.
Great universal Teacher! he shall mould
Thy spirit, and by giving make it ask.

Therefore all seasons shall be sweet to thee,
Whether the summer clothe the general earth
With greenness, or the redbreast sit and sing
Betwixt the tufts of snow on the bare branch
Of mossy apple-tree, while the nigh thatch
Smokes in the sun-thaw; whether the eave-drops fall
Heard only in the trances of the blast,
Or if the secret ministry of frost
Shall hang them up in silent icicles,
Quietly shining to the quiet Moon.

France: An Ode

I

Ye Clouds! that far above me float and pause,
   Whose pathless march no mortal may controul!
   Ye Ocean-Waves! that, wheresoe'er ye roll,
Yield homage only to eternal laws!
Ye Woods! that listen to the night-birds singing,
   Midway the smooth and perilous slope reclined,
Save when your own imperious branches swinging,
   Have made a solemn music of the wind!
Where, like a man beloved of God,
Through glooms, which never woodman trod,
     How oft, pursuing fancies holy,
My moonlight way o'er flowering weeds I wound,
     Inspired, beyond the guess of folly,
By each rude shape and wild unconquerable sound!
O ye loud Waves! and O ye Forests high!
   And O ye Clouds that far above me soared!
Thou rising Sun! thou blue rejoicing Sky!
   Yea, every thing that is and will be free!
   Bear witness for me, wheresoe'er ye be,
   With what deep worship I have still adored
     The spirit of divinest Liberty.

II

When France in wrath her giant-limbs upreared,
   And with that oath, which smote air, earth, and sea,
   Stamped her strong foot and said she would be free,
Bear witness for me, how I hoped and feared!
With what a joy my lofty gratulation
   Unawed I sang, amid a slavish band:
And when to whelm the disenchanted nation,
   Like fiends embattled by a wizard's wand,
     The Monarchs marched in evil day,
     And Britain joined the dire array;
   Though dear her shores and circling ocean,
Though many friendships, many youthful loves

Had swoln the patriot emotion
And flung a magic light o'er all her hills and groves;
Yet still my voice, unaltered, sang defeat
    To all that braved the tyrant-quelling lance,
And shame too long delayed and vain retreat!
For ne'er, O Liberty! with partial aim
I dimmed thy light or damped thy holy flame;
    But blessed the paeans of delivered France,
And hung my head and wept at Britain's name.

III

'And what,' I said, 'though Blasphemy's loud scream
    With that sweet music of deliverance strove!
    Though all the fierce and drunken passions wove
A dance more wild than e'er was maniac's dream!
    Ye storms, that round the dawning East assembled,
The Sun was rising, though ye hid his light!'
    And when, to soothe my soul, that hoped and trembled,
The dissonance ceased, and all seemed calm and bright;
    When France her front deep-scarr'd and gory
    Concealed with clustering wreaths of glory;
        When, insupportably advancing,
    Her arm made mockery of the warrior's ramp;
        While timid looks of fury glancing,
    Domestic treason, crushed beneath her fatal stamp,
Writhed like a wounded dragon in his gore;
    Then I reproached my fears that would not flee;
'And soon,' I said, 'shall Wisdom teach her lore
In the low huts of them that toil and groan!
And, conquering by her happiness alone,
    Shall France compel the nations to be free,
Till Love and Joy look round, and call the Earth their own.'

IV

Forgive me, Freedom! O forgive those dreams!
    I hear thy voice, I hear thy loud lament,
    From bleak Helvetia's icy caverns sent —
I hear thy groans upon her blood-stained streams!
    Heroes, that for your peaceful country perished,
And ye that, fleeing, spot your mountain-snows

With bleeding wounds; forgive me, that I cherished
One thought that ever blessed your cruel foes!
   To scatter rage, and traitorous guilt,
   Where Peace her jealous home had built;
     A patriot-race to disinherit
Of all that made their stormy wilds so dear;
     And with inexpiable spirit
To taint the bloodless freedom of the mountaineer —
O France, that mockest Heaven, adulterous, blind,
   And patriot only in pernicious toils!
Are these thy boasts, Champion of human kind?
   To mix with Kings in the low lust of sway,
Yell in the hunt, and share the murderous prey;
To insult the shrine of Liberty with spoils
   From freemen torn; to tempt and to betray?

V

   The Sensual and the Dark rebel in vain,
   Slaves by their own compulsion! In mad game
   They burst their manacles and wear the name
     Of Freedom, graven on a heavier chain!
   O Liberty! with profitless endeavour
Have I pursued thee, many a weary hour;
   But thou nor swell'st the victor's strain, nor ever
Didst breathe thy soul in forms of human power.
   Alike from all, howe'er they praise thee,
     (Nor prayer, nor boastful name delays thee)
     Alike from Priestcraft's harpy minions,
   And factious Blasphemy's obscener slaves,
     Thou speedest on thy subtle pinions,
The guide of homeless winds, and playmate of the waves!
And there I felt thee! — on that sea-cliff's verge,
   Whose pines, scarce travelled by the breeze above,
Had made one murmur with the distant surge!
Yes, while I stood and gazed, my temples bare,
And shot my being through earth, sea, and air,
   Possessing all things with intensest love,
     O Liberty! my spirit felt thee there.

Kubla Khan

In Xanadu did Kubla Khan
A stately pleasure-dome decree:
Where Alph, the sacred river, ran
Through caverns measureless to man
   Down to a sunless sea.
So twice five miles of fertile ground
With walls and towers were girdled round:
And there were gardens bright with sinuous rills,
Where blossomed many an incense-bearing tree;
And here were forests ancient as the hills,
Enfolding sunny spots of greenery.

But oh! that deep romantic chasm which slanted
Down the green hill athwart a cedarn cover!
A savage place! as holy and enchanted
As e'er beneath a waning moon was haunted
By woman wailing for her demon-lover!
And from this chasm, with ceaseless turmoil seething,
As if this earth in fast thick pants were breathing,
A mighty fountain momently was forced:
Amid whose swift half-intermitted burst
Huge fragments vaulted like rebounding hail,
Or chaffy grain beneath the thresher's flail:
And 'mid these dancing rocks at once and ever
It flung up momently the sacred river.
Five miles meandering with a mazy motion
Through wood and dale the sacred river ran,
Then reached the caverns measureless to man,
And sank in tumult to a lifeless ocean:
And 'mid this tumult Kubla heard from far
Ancestral voices prophesying war!
   The shadow of the dome of pleasure
   Floated midway on the waves;
   Where was heard the mingled measure
   From the fountain and the caves.
It was a miracle of rare device,
A sunny pleasure-dome with caves of ice!

A damsel with a dulcimer
In a vision once I saw:
It was an Abyssinian maid,
And on her dulcimer she played,
Singing of Mount Abora.
Could I revive within me
Her symphony and song,
To such a deep delight 'twould win me,
That with music loud and long,
I would build that dome in air,
That sunny dome! those caves of ice!
And all who heard should see them there,
And all should cry, Beware! Beware!
His flashing eyes, his floating hair!
Weave a circle round him thrice,
And close your eyes with holy dread,
For he on honey-dew hath fed,
And drunk the milk of Paradise.

Dejection: An Ode

Late, late yestreen I saw the new Moon,
With the old Moon in her arms;
And I fear, I fear, my Master dear!
We shall have a deadly storm.
> *Ballad of Sir Patrick Spence.*

I   Well! If the Bard was weather-wise, who made
     The grand old ballad of Sir Patrick Spence,
     This night, so tranquil now, will not go hence
Unroused by winds, that ply a busier trade
Than those which mould yon cloud in lazy flakes,
Or the dull sobbing draft, that moans and rakes
Upon the strings of this Æolian lute,
     Which better far were mute.
   For lo! the New-moon winter-bright!
   And overspread with phantom light,
     (With swimming phantom light o'erspread

But rimmed and circled by a silver thread)
I see the old Moon in her lap, foretelling
  The coming-on of rain and squally blast.
  And oh! that even now the gust were swelling,
    And the slant night-shower driving loud and fast!
Those sounds which oft have raised me, whilst they awed,
    And sent my soul abroad,
Might now perhaps their wonted impulse give,
Might startle this dull pain, and make it move and live!

II A grief without a pang, void, dark, and drear,
    A stifled, drowsy, unimpassioned grief,
      Which finds no natural outlet, no relief,
        In word, or sigh, or tear —
O Lady! in this wan and heartless mood,
To other thoughts by yonder throstle woo'd,
  All this long eve, so balmy and serene,
Have I been gazing on the western sky,
  And its peculiar tint of yellow green:
And still I gaze — and with how blank an eye!
And those thin clouds above, in flakes and bars,
That give away their motion to the stars;
Those stars, that glide behind them or between,
Now sparkling, now bedimmed, but always seen:
Yon crescent Moon, as fixed as if it grew
In its own cloudless, starless lake of blue;
I see them all so excellently fair,
I see, not feel, how beautiful they are!

III   My genial spirits fail;
      And what can these avail
To lift the smothering weight from off my breast?
    It were a vain endeavour,
      Though I should gaze for ever
On that green light that lingers in the west:
I may not hope from outward forms to win
The passion and the life, whose fountains are within.

IV O Lady! we receive but what we give,
And in our life alone does Nature live:

Ours is her wedding garment, ours her shroud!
　And would we aught behold, of higher worth,
Than that inanimate cold world allowed
To the poor loveless ever-anxious crowd,
　　Ah! from the soul itself must issue forth
A light, a glory, a fair luminous cloud
　　　Enveloping the Earth —
And from the soul itself must there be sent
　A sweet and potent voice, of its own birth,
Of all sweet sounds the life and element!

V　O pure of heart! thou need'st not ask of me
What this strong music in the soul may be!
What, and wherein it doth exist,
This light, this glory, this fair luminous mist,
This beautiful and beauty-making power.
　　Joy, virtuous Lady! Joy that ne'er was given,
Save to the pure, and in their purest hour,
Life, and Life's effluence, cloud at once and shower,
Joy, Lady! is the spirit and the power,
Which wedding Nature to us gives in dower
　A new Earth and new Heaven,
Undreamt of by the sensual and the proud —
Joy is the sweet voice, Joy the luminous cloud —
　　We in ourselves rejoice!
And thence flows all that charms or ear or sight,
　All melodies the echoes of that voice,
All colours a suffusion from that light.

VI　There was a time when, though my path was rough,
　　This joy within me dallied with distress,
And all misfortunes were but as the stuff
　　Whence Fancy made me dreams of happiness:
For hope grew round me, like the twining vine,
And fruits, and foliage, not my own, seemed mine.
But now afflictions bow me down to earth:
Nor care I that they rob me of my mirth;
　　　But oh! each visitation

Suspends what nature gave me at my birth,
  My shaping spirit of Imagination.
For not to think of what I needs must feel,
  But to be still and patient, all I can;
And haply by abstruse research to steal
  From my own nature all the natural man —
  This was my sole resource, my only plan:
Till that which suits a part infects the whole,
And now is almost grown the habit of my soul.

VII Hence, viper thoughts, that coil around my mind,
      Reality's dark dream!
I turn from you, and listen to the wind,
  Which long has raved unnoticed. What a scream
Of agony by torture lengthened out
That lute sent forth! Thou Wind, that rav'st without,
  Bare crag, or mountain-tairn, or blasted tree,
Or pine-grove whither woodman never clomb,
Or lonely house, long held the witches' home,
  Methinks were fitter instruments for thee,
Mad Lutanist! who in this month of showers,
Of dark-brown gardens, and of peeping flowers,
Mak'st Devils' yule, with worse than wintry song,
The blossoms, buds, and timorous leaves among.
  Thou Actor, perfect in all tragic sounds!
Thou mighty Poet, e'en to frenzy bold!
    What tell'st thou now about?
    'Tis of the rushing of an host in rout,
  With groans, of trampled men, with smarting wounds —
At once they groan with pain, and shudder with the cold!
But hush! there is a pause of deepest silence!
  And all that noise, as of a rushing crowd,
With groans, and tremulous shudderings — all is over —
  It tells another tale, with sounds less deep and loud!
    A tale of less affright,
    And tempered with delight,
As Otway's self had framed the tender lay, —
    'Tis of a little child
    Upon a lonesome wild,

Not far from home, but she hath lost her way:
And now moans low in bitter grief and fear,
And now screams loud, and hopes to make her mother hear.

VIII   'Tis midnight, but small thoughts have I of sleep:
Full seldom may my friend such vigils keep!
Visit her, gentle Sleep! with wings of healing,
    And may this storm be but a mountain-birth,
May all the stars hang bright above her dwelling,
    Silent as though they watched the sleeping Earth!
        With light heart may she rise,
        Gay fancy, cheerful eyes,
    Joy lift her spirit, joy attune her voice;
To her may all things live, from pole to pole,
Their life the eddying of her living soul!
    O simple spirit, guided from above,
Dear Lady! friend devoutest of my choice,
Thus mayest thou ever, evermore rejoice.

The Pains of Sleep

Ere on my bed my limbs I lay,
It hath not been my use to pray
With moving lips or bended knees;
But silently, by slow degrees,
My spirit I to Love compose,
In humble trust mine eye-lids close,
With reverential resignation,
No wish conceived, no thought exprest,
Only a sense of supplication;
A sense o'er all my soul imprest
That I am weak, yet not unblest,
Since in me, round me, every where
Eternal Strength and Wisdom are.

But yester-night I prayed aloud
In anguish and in agony,

Up-starting from the fiendish crowd
Of shapes and thoughts that tortured me:
A lurid light, a trampling throng,
Sense of intolerable wrong,
And whom I scorned, those only strong!
Thirst of revenge, the powerless will
Still baffled, and yet burning still!
Desire with loathing strangely mixed
On wild or hateful objects fixed.
Fantastic passions! maddening brawl!
And shame and terror over all!
Deeds to be hid which were not hid,
Which all confused I could not know
Whether I suffered, or I did:
For all seemed guilt, remorse or woe,
My own or others still the same
Life-stifling fear, soul-stifling shame.

So two nights passed: the night's dismay
Saddened and stunned the coming day.
Sleep, the wide blessing, seemed to me
Distemper's worst calamity.
The third night, when my own loud scream
Had waked me from the fiendish dream,
O'ercome with sufferings strange and wild,
I wept as I had been a child;
And having thus by tears subdued
My anguish to a milder mood,
Such punishments, I said, were due
To natures deepliest stained with sin, —
For aye entempesting anew
The unfathomable hell within,
The horror of their deeds to view,
To know and loathe, yet wish and do!
Such griefs with such men well agree,
But wherefore, wherefore fall on me?
To be beloved is all I need,
And whom I love, I love indeed.

GEORGE GORDON, LORD BYRON
(1788–1824)

"When we two parted"

When we two parted
  In silence and tears,
Half broken-hearted
  To sever for years,
Pale grew thy cheek and cold,
  Colder thy kiss;
Truly that hour foretold
  Sorrow to this.

The dew of the morning
  Sunk chill on my brow —
It felt like the warning
  Of what I feel now.
Thy vows are all broken,
  And light is thy fame;
I hear thy name spoken,
  And share in its shame.

They name thee before me,
  A knell to mine ear;
A shudder comes o'er me —
  Why wert thou so dear?
They know not I knew thee,
  Who knew thee too well: —
Long, long shall I rue thee,
  Too deeply to tell.

In secret we met —
  In silence I grieve
That thy heart could forget,
  Thy spirit deceive.
If I should meet thee
  After long years,
How should I greet thee? —
  With silence and tears.

The Girl of Cadiz

Oh never talk again to me
　　Of northern climes and British ladies;
It has not been your lot to see,
　　Like me, the lovely girl of Cadiz.
Although her eye be not of blue,
　　Nor fair her locks, like English lasses,
How far its own expressive hue
　　The languid azure eye surpasses!

Prometheus-like, from heaven she stole
　　The fire, that through those silken lashes
In darkest glances seems to roll,
　　From eyes that cannot hide their flashes:
And as along her bosom steal
　　In lengthen'd flow her raven tresses,
You'd swear each clustering lock could feel,
　　And curl'd to give her neck caresses.

Our English maids are long to woo,
　　And frigid even in possession;
And if their charms be fair to view,
　　Their lips are slow at Love's confession:
But, born beneath a brighter sun,
　　For love ordain'd the Spanish maid is,
And who, — when fondly, fairly won, —
　　Enchants you like the Girl of Cadiz?

The Spanish maid is no coquette,
　　Nor joys to see a lover tremble,
And if she love, or if she hate,
　　Alike she knows not to dissemble.
Her heart can ne'er be bought or sold —
　　Howe'er it beats, it beats sincerely;
And, though it will not bend to gold,
　　'Twill love you long and love you dearly.

The Spanish girl that meets your love
　　Ne'er taunts you with a mock denial,
For every thought is bent to prove
　　Her passion in the hour of trial.

When thronging foemen menace Spain,
    She dares the deed and shares the danger;
And should her lover press the plain,
    She hurls the spear, her love's avenger.

And when, beneath the evening star,
    She mingles in the gay Bolero,
Or sings to her attuned guitar
    Of Christian knight or Moorish hero,
Or counts her beads with fairy hand
    Beneath the twinkling rays of Hesper,
Or joins Devotion's choral band,
    To chaunt the sweet and hallow'd vesper; —

In each her charms the heart must move
    Of all who venture to behold her;
Then let not maids less fair reprove
    Because her bosom is not colder:
Through many a clime 'tis mine to roam
    Where many a soft and melting maid is,
But none abroad, and few at home,
    May match the dark-eyed Girl of Cadiz.

"She walks in beauty"

She walks in beauty, like the night
    Of cloudless climes and starry skies;
And all that's best of dark and bright
    Meet in her aspect and her eyes:
Thus mellow'd to that tender light
    Which heaven to gaudy day denies.

One shade the more, one ray the less,
    Had half impair'd the nameless grace
Which waves in every raven tress,
    Or softly lightens o'er her face;
Where thoughts serenely sweet express
    How pure, how dear their dwelling-place.

And on that cheek, and o'er that brow,
    So soft, so calm, yet eloquent,
The smiles that win, the tints that glow,
    But tell of days in goodness spent,
A mind at peace with all below,
    A heart whose love is innocent!

The Destruction of Sennacherib

The Assyrian came down like the wolf on the fold,
And his cohorts were gleaming in purple and gold;
And the sheen of their spears was like stars on the sea,
When the blue wave rolls nightly on deep Galilee.

Like the leaves of the forest when Summer is green,
That host with their banners at sunset were seen:
Like the leaves of the forest when Autumn hath blown,
That host on the morrow lay wither'd and strown.

For the Angel of Death spread his wings on the blast,
And breathed in the face of the foe as he pass'd;
And the eyes of the sleepers wax'd deadly and chill,
And their hearts but once heaved, and for ever grew still!

And there lay the steed with his nostril all wide,
But through it there roll'd not the breath of his pride:
And the foam of his gasping lay white on the turf,
And cold as the spray of the rock-beating surf.

And there lay the rider distorted and pale,
With the dew on his brow and the rust on his mail;
And the tents were all silent, the banners alone,
The lances unlifted, the trumpet unblown.

And the widows of Ashur are loud in their wail,
And the idols are broke in the temple of Baal;

And the might of the Gentile, unsmote by the sword,
Hath melted like snow in the glance of the Lord!

Stanzas for Music

There be none of Beauty's daughters
    With a magic like thee;
And like music on the waters
    Is thy sweet voice to me:
When, as if its sound were causing
The charmèd ocean's pausing,
The waves lie still and gleaming,
And the lull'd winds seem dreaming.

And the midnight moon is weaving
    Her bright chain o'er the deep;
Whose breast is gently heaving,
    As an infant's asleep:
So the spirit bows before thee,
To listen and adore thee;
With a full but soft emotion,
Like the swell of Summer's ocean.

The Prisoner of Chillon

A FABLE

SONNET ON CHILLON

Eternal Spirit of the chainless Mind!
    Brightest in dungeons, Liberty! thou art,
    For there thy habitation is the heart —
The heart which love of thee alone can bind;
And when thy sons to fetters are consign'd —

To fetters, and the damp vault's dayless gloom,
  Their country conquers with their martyrdom,
And Freedom's fame finds wings on every wind.
Chillon! thy prison is a holy place,
  And thy sad floor an altar; for 'twas trod,
Until his very steps have left a trace
  Worn, as if thy cold pavement were a sod,
By Bonnivard!* — May none those marks efface!
  For they appeal from tyranny to God.

I

My hair is grey, but not with years,
    Nor grew it white
    In a single night,
As men's have grown from sudden fears.
My limbs are bow'd, though not with toil,
  But rusted with a vile repose,
For they have been a dungeon's spoil,
  And mine has been the fate of those
To whom the goodly earth and air
Are bann'd, and barr'd — forbidden fare.
But this was for my father's faith,
I suffer'd chains and courted death;
That father perish'd at the stake
For tenets he would not forsake;
And for the same his lineal race
In darkness found a dwelling-place.
We were seven — who now are one,
  Six in youth, and one in age,
Finish'd as they had begun,
  Proud of Persecution's rage;
One in fire, and two in field,
Their belief with blood have seal'd,
Dying as their father died,
For the God their foes denied;
Three were in a dungeon cast,
Of whom this wreck is left the last.

---

*François de Bonnivard (1496–1570), imprisoned in the Château de Chillon (at the eastern end of the Lake of Geneva) for his defense of the freedom of Geneva.

II

There are seven pillars of Gothic mould
In Chillon's dungeons deep and old,
There are seven columns, massy and grey,
Dim with a dull imprison'd ray,
A sunbeam which hath lost its way,
And through the crevice and the cleft
Of the thick wall is fallen and left;
Creeping o'er the floor so damp,
Like a marsh's meteor lamp.
And in each pillar there is a ring,
    And in each ring there is a chain;
That iron is a cankering thing,
    For in these limbs its teeth remain,
With marks that will not wear away,
Till I have done with this new day,
Which now is painful to these eyes,
Which have not seen the sun so rise
For years — I cannot count them o'er,
I lost their long and heavy score
When my last brother droop'd and died,
And I lay living by his side.

III

They chain'd us each to a column stone,
And we were three — yet, each alone;
We could not move a single pace,
We could not see each other's face,
But with that pale and livid light
That made us strangers in our sight.
And thus together, yet apart,
Fetter'd in hand, but join'd in heart,
'Twas still some solace, in the dearth
Of the pure elements of earth,
To hearken to each other's speech,
And each turn comforter to each
With some new hope or legend old,
Or song heroically bold;
But even these at length grew cold.

Our voices took a dreary tone,
An echo of the dungeon stone,
    A grating sound — not full and free
    As they of yore were wont to be:
    It might be fancy, but to me
They never sounded like our own.

IV

I was the eldest of the three,
    And to uphold and cheer the rest
    I ought to do — and did my best;
And each did well in his degree.
    The youngest, whom my father loved,
Because our mother's brow was given
To him, with eyes as blue as heaven —
    For him my soul was sorely moved.
And truly might it be distress'd
To see such bird in such a nest;
For he was beautiful as day
    (When day was beautiful to me
    As to young eagles being free) —
    A polar day, which will not see
A sunset till its summer's gone,
    Its sleepless summer of long light,
The snow-clad offspring of the sun:
    And thus he was as pure and bright,
And in his natural spirit gay,
With tears for nought but others' ills;
And then they flow'd like mountain rills,
Unless he could assuage the woe
Which he abhorr'd to view below.

V

The other was as pure of mind,
But form'd to combat with his kind;
Strong in his frame, and of a mood
Which 'gainst the world in war had stood,
And perish'd in the foremost rank
    With joy: — but not in chains to pine:

His spirit wither'd with their clank,
  I saw it silently decline —
  And so perchance in sooth did mine:
But yet I forced it on to cheer
Those relics of a home so dear.
He was a hunter of the hills,
  Had follow'd there the deer and wolf;
  To him this dungeon was a gulf,
And fetter'd feet the worst of ills.

VI

  Lake Leman lies by Chillon's walls:
A thousand feet in depth below
Its massy waters meet and flow;
Thus much the fathom-line was sent
From Chillon's snow-white battlement
  Which round about the wave inthrals:
A double dungeon wall and wave
Have made — and like a living grave.
Below the surface of the lake
The dark vault lies wherein we lay:
We heard it ripple night and day;
  Sounding o'er our heads it knock'd;
And I have felt the winter's spray
Wash through the bars when winds were high
And wanton in the happy sky;
  And then the very rock hath rock'd,
  And I have felt it shake, unshock'd,
Because I could have smiled to see
The death that would have set me free.

VII

I said my nearer brother pined,
I said his mighty heart declined,
He loathed and put away his food;
It was not that 'twas coarse and rude,
For we were used to hunters' fare,
And for the like had little care.
The milk drawn from the mountain goat
Was changed for water from the moat,

Our bread was such as captives' tears
Have moisten'd many a thousand years,
Since man first pent his fellow men
Like brutes within an iron den;
But what were these to us or him?
These wasted not his heart or limb;
My brother's soul was of that mould
Which in a palace had grown cold,
Had his free breathing been denied
The range of the steep mountain's side.
Buy why delay the truth? — he died.
I saw, and could not hold his head,
Nor reach his dying hand — nor dead, —
Though hard I strove, but strove in vain,
To rend and gnash my bonds in twain.
He died — and they unlock'd his chain,
And scoop'd for him a shallow grave
Even from the cold earth of our cave.
I begg'd them, as a boon, to lay
His corse in dust whereon the day
Might shine — it was a foolish thought,
But then within my brain it wrought,
That even in death his freeborn breast
In such a dungeon could not rest.
I might have spared my idle prayer;
They coldly laugh'd — and laid him there:
The flat and turfless earth above
The being we so much did love;
His empty chain above it leant,
Such murder's fitting monument!

VIII

But he, the favourite and the flower,
Most cherish'd since his natal hour,
His mother's image in fair face,
The infant love of all his race,
His martyr'd father's dearest thought,
My latest care, for whom I sought
To hoard my life, that his might be
Less wretched now, and one day free;

He, too, who yet had held untired
A spirit natural or inspired —
He, too, was struck, and day by day
Was wither'd on the stalk away.
Oh, God! it is a fearful thing
To see the human soul take wing
In any shape, in any mood: —
I've seen it rushing forth in blood,
I've seen it on the breaking ocean
Strive with a swoln convulsive motion,
I've seen the sick and ghastly bed
Of Sin delirious with its dread:
But these were horrors — this was woe
Unmix'd with such — but sure and slow.
He faded, and so calm and meek,
So softly worn, so sweetly weak,
So tearless, yet so tender — kind,
And grieved for those he left behind;
With all the while a cheek whose bloom
Was as a mockery of the tomb,
Whose tints as gently sunk away
As a departing rainbow's ray;
An eye of most transparent light,
That almost made the dungeon bright;
And not a word of murmur, not
A groan o'er his untimely lot, —
A little talk of better days,
A little hope my own to raise,
For I was sunk in silence — lost
In this last loss, of all the most;
And then the sighs he would suppress
Of fainting nature's feebleness,
More slowly drawn, grew less and less.
I listen'd, but I could not hear —
I call'd, for I was wild with fear;
I knew 'twas hopeless, but my dread
Would not be thus admonishèd.
I call'd, and thought I heard a sound —
I burst my chain with one strong bound,
And rush'd to him: — I found him not,
I only stirr'd in this black spot,

I only lived — *I* only drew
The accursèd breath of dungeon-dew;
The last — the sole — the dearest link
Between me and the eternal brink,
Which bound me to my failing race,
Was broken in this fatal place.
One on the earth, and one beneath —
My brothers — both had ceased to breathe:
I took that hand which lay so still,
Alas! my own was full as chill,
I had not strength to stir, or strive,
But felt that I was still alive —
A frantic feeling, when we know
That what we love shall ne'er be so.
  I know not why
  I could not die,
I had no earthly hope — but faith,
And that forbade a selfish death.

IX

What next befell me then and there
 I know not well — I never knew;
First came the loss of light, and air,
 And then of darkness too.
I had no thought, no feeling — none —
Among the stones I stood a stone,
And was, scarce conscious what I wist,
As shrubless crags within the mist;
For all was blank, and bleak, and grey,
It was not night — it was not day,
It was not even the dungeon-light
So hateful to my heavy sight,
But vacancy absorbing space,
And fixedness — without a place;
There were no stars, no earth, no time,
No check, no change, no good, no crime —
But silence, and a stirless breath
Which neither was of life nor death;
A sea of stagnant idleness,
Blind, boundless, mute, and motionless!

X

A light broke in upon my brain, —
    It was the carol of a bird;
It ceased, and then it came again,
    The sweetest song ear ever heard,
And mine was thankful till my eyes
Ran over with the glad surprise,
And they that moment could not see
I was the mate of misery.
But then by dull degrees came back
My senses to their wonted track;
I saw the dungeon walls and floor
Close slowly round me as before,
I saw the glimmer of the sun
Creeping as it before had done, -
But through the crevice where it came
That bird was perch'd, as fond and tame,
    And tamer than upon the tree;
A lovely bird, with azure wings,
And song that said a thousand things,
    And seem'd to say them all for me!
I never saw its like before,
I ne'er shall see its likeness more:
It seem'd like me to want a mate,
But was not half so desolate,
And it was come to love me when
None lived to love me so again,
And cheering from my dungeon's brink,
Had brought me back to feel and think.
I know not if it late were free,
    Or broke its cage to perch on mine,
But knowing well captivity,
    Sweet bird! I could not wish for thine!
Or if it were, in wingèd guise,
A visitant from Paradise;
For — Heaven forgive that thought! the while
Which made me both to weep and smile —
I sometimes deem'd that it might be
My brother's soul come down to me;
But then at last away it flew,

And then 'twas mortal — well I knew,
For he would never thus have flown,
And left me twice so doubly lone, —
Lone — as the corse within its shroud,
Lone — as a solitary cloud,
  A single cloud on a sunny day,
While all the rest of heaven is clear,
A frown upon the atmosphere
That hath no business to appear
  When skies are blue and earth is gay.

XI

A kind of change came in my fate,
My keepers grew compassionate;
I know not what had made them so,
They were inured to sights of woe,
But so it was: — my broken chain
With links unfasten'd did remain,
And it was liberty to stride
Along my cell from side to side,
And up and down, and then athwart,
And tread it over every part;
And round the pillars one by one,
Returning where my walk begun,
Avoiding only, as I trod,
My brothers' graves without a sod;
For if I thought with heedless tread
My step profaned their lowly bed,
My breath came gaspingly and thick,
And my crush'd heart fell blind and sick.

XII

I made a footing in the wall,
  It was not therefrom to escape,
For I had buried one and all
  Who loved me in a human shape;
And the whole earth would henceforth be
A wider prison unto me.
No child, no sire, no kin had I,

No partner in my misery;
I thought of this, and I was glad,
For thought of them had made me mad;
But I was curious to ascend
To my barr'd windows, and to bend
Once more, upon the mountains high,
The quiet of a loving eye.

XIII

I saw them — and they were the same,
They were not changed like me in frame;
I saw their thousand years of snow
On high — their wide long lake below,
And the blue Rhone in fullest flow;
I heard the torrents leap and gush
O'er channell'd rock and broken bush;
I saw the white-wall'd distant town,
And whiter sails go skimming down.
And then there was a little isle,
Which in my very face did smile,
    The only one in view;
A small green isle, it seem'd no more,
Scarce broader than my dungeon floor,
But in it there were three tall trees,
And o'er it blew the mountain breeze,
And by it there were waters flowing,
And on it there were young flowers growing
    Of gentle breath and hue.
The fish swam by the castle wall,
And they seem'd joyous each and all;
The eagle rode the rising blast,
Methought he never flew so fast
As then to me he seem'd to fly;
And then new tears came in my eye,
And I felt troubled and would fain
I had not left my recent chain.
And when I did descend again,
The darkness of my dim abode
Fell on me as a heavy load;
It was as is a new-dug grave,
Closing o'er one we sought to save;
And yet my glance, too much oppress'd,
Had almost need of such a rest.

XIV

It might be months, or years, or days —
   I kept no count, I took no note,
I had no hope my eyes to raise,
   And clear them of their dreary mote.
At last men came to set me free,
   I ask'd not why, and reck'd not where,
It was at length the same to me,
Fetter'd or fetterless to be,
   I learn'd to love despair.
And thus when they appear'd at last,
And all my bonds aside were cast,
These heavy walls to me had grown
A hermitage — and all my own!
And half I felt as they were come
To tear me from a second home.
With spiders I had friendship made,
And watch'd them in their sullen trade,
Had seen the mice by moonlight play,
And why should I feel less than they?
We were all inmates of one place,
And I, the monarch of each race,
Had power to kill — yet, strange to tell!
In quiet we had learn'd to dwell —
My very chains and I grew friends,
So much a long communion tends
To make us what we are: — even I
Regain'd my freedom with a sigh.

Darkness

I had a dream, which was not all a dream.
The bright sun was extinguish'd, and the stars
Did wander darkling in the eternal space,
Rayless, and pathless, and the icy earth
Swung blind and blackening in the moonless air;
Morn came and went — and came, and brought no day,
And men forgot their passions in the dead

Of this their desolation; and all hearts
Were chill'd into a selfish prayer for light.
And they did live by watch fires — and the thrones,
The palaces of crownèd kings — the huts,
The habitations of all things which dwell,
Were burnt for beacons; cities were consumed,
And men were gather'd round their blazing homes
To look once more into each other's face.
Happy were those who dwelt within the eye
Of the volcanos, and their mountain-torch:
A fearful hope was all the world contain'd;
Forests were set on fire — but hour by hour
They fell and faded — and the crackling trunks
Extinguish'd with a crash — and all was black.
The brows of men by the despairing light
Wore an unearthly aspect, as by fits
The flashes fell upon them; some lay down
And hid their eyes and wept; and some did rest
Their chins upon their clenchèd hands, and smiled;
And others hurried to and fro, and fed
Their funeral piles with fuel, and look'd up
With mad disquietude on the dull sky,
The pall of a past world; and then again
With curses cast them down upon the dust,
And gnash'd their teeth and howl'd. The wild birds shriek'd,
And, terrified, did flutter on the ground,
And flap their useless wings; the wildest brutes
Came tame and tremulous; and vipers crawl'd
And twined themselves among the multitude,
Hissing, but stingless — they were slain for food.
And War, which for a moment was no more,
Did glut himself again; — a meal was bought
With blood, and each sate sullenly apart
Gorging himself in gloom. No love was left;
All earth was but one thought — and that was death,
Immediate and inglorious; and the pang
Of famine fed upon all entrails — men
Died, and their bones were tombless as their flesh;
The meagre by the meagre were devour'd,
Even dogs assail'd their masters, all save one,

And he was faithful to a corse, and kept
The birds and beasts and famish'd men at bay,
Till hunger clung them, or the dropping dead
Lured their lank jaws. Himself sought out no food,
But with a piteous and perpetual moan,
And a quick desolate cry, licking the hand
Which answer'd not with a caress — he died.
The crowd was famish'd by degrees; but two
Of an enormous city did survive,
And they were enemies. They met beside
The dying embers of an altar-place,
Where had been heap'd a mass of holy things
For an unholy usage; they raked up,
And shivering scraped with their cold skeleton hands
The feeble ashes, and their feeble breath
Blew for a little life, and made a flame
Which was a mockery. Then they lifted up
Their eyes as it grew lighter, and beheld
Each other's aspects — saw, and shriek'd, and died —
Even of their mutual hideousness they died,
Unknowing who he was upon whose brow
Famine had written Fiend. The world was void,
The populous and the powerful was a lump,
Seasonless, herbless, treeless, manless, lifeless —
A lump of death — a chaos of hard clay.
The rivers, lakes, and ocean all stood still,
And nothing stirr'd within their silent depths;
Ships sailorless lay rotting on the sea,
And their masts fell down piecemeal: as they dropp'd
They slept on the abyss without a surge —
The waves were dead; the tides were in their grave,
The Moon, their mistress, had expired before;
The winds were wither'd in the stagnant air,
And the clouds perish'd; Darkness had no need
Of aid from them — She was the Universe.

Stanzas to Augusta

Though the day of my destiny's over,
   And the star of my fate hath declined,
Thy soft heart refused to discover
   The faults which so many could find;
Though thy soul with my grief was acquainted,
   It shrunk not to share it with me,
And the love which my spirit hath painted
   It never hath found but in *thee*.

Then when nature around me is smiling,
   The last smile which answers to mine,
I do not believe it beguiling,
   Because it reminds me of thine;
And when winds are at war with the ocean,
   As the breasts I believed in with me,
If their billows excite an emotion,
   It is that they bear me from *thee*.

Though the rock of my last hope is shiver'd,
   And its fragments are sunk in the wave,
Though I feel that my soul is deliver'd
   To pain — it shall not be its slave.
There is many a pang to pursue me:
   They may crush, but they shall not contemn —
They may torture, but shall not subdue me —
   'Tis of *thee* that I think — not of them.

Though human, thou didst not deceive me,
   Though woman, thou didst not forsake,
Though loved, thou forborest to grieve me,
   Though slander'd, thou never couldst shake, —
Though trusted, thou didst not disclaim me,
   Though parted, it was not to fly,
Though watchful, 'twas not to defame me,
   Nor, mute, that the world might belie.

Yet I blame not the world, nor despise it,
   Nor the war of the many with one —
If my soul was not fitted to prize it,
   'Twas folly not sooner to shun:
And if dearly that error hath cost me,
   And more than I once could foresee,
I have found that, whatever it lost me,
   It could not deprive me of *thee*.

From the wreck of the past, which hath perish'd,
   Thus much I at least may recall,
It hath taught me that what I most cherish'd
   Deserved to be dearest of all:
In the desert a fountain is springing,
   In the wide waste there still is a tree,
And a bird in the solitude singing,
   Which speaks to my spirit of *thee*.

"So we'll go no more a roving"

So we'll go no more a roving
   So late into the night,
Though the heart be still as loving,
   And the moon be still as bright.

For the sword outwears its sheath,
   And the soul wears out the breast,
And the heart must pause to breathe,
   And Love itself have rest.

Though the night was made for loving,
   And the day returns too soon,
Yet we'll go no more a roving
   By the light of the moon.

"Childe Harold's Pilgrimage":
"Adieu, adieu! my native shore" (Canto I)

1 'Adieu, adieu! my native shore
       Fades o'er the waters blue;
   The Night-winds sigh, the breakers roar,
       And shrieks the wild sea-mew.
   Yon Sun that sets upon the sea
       We follow in his flight;
   Farewell awhile to him and thee,
       My native Land — Good Night!

2 'A few short hours and He will rise
       To give the Morrow birth;
   And I shall hail the main and skies,
       But not my mother Earth.
   Deserted is my own good hall,
       Its hearth is desolate;
   Wild weeds are gathering on the wall;
       My dog howls at the gate.

3 'Come hither, hither, my little page!
       Why dost thou weep and wail?
   Or dost thou dread the billows' rage,
       Or tremble at the gale?
   But dash the tear-drop from thine eye;
       Our ship is swift and strong,
   Our fleetest falcon scarce can fly
       More merrily along.' —

4 'Let winds be shrill, let waves roll high,
       I fear not wave nor wind;
   Yet marvel not, Sir Childe, that I
       Am sorrowful in mind;
   For I have from my father gone,
       A mother whom I love,
   And have no friend, save these alone,
       But thee — and one above.

5 'My father bless'd me fervently,
       Yet did not much complain;

But sorely will my mother sigh
  Till I come back again.' —
'Enough, enough, my little lad!
  Such tears become thine eye;
If I thy guileless bosom had,
  Mine own would not be dry. —

6 'Come hither, hither, my staunch yeoman,
     Why dost thou look so pale?
Or dost thou dread a French foeman?
     Or shiver at the gale?' —
'Deem'st thou I tremble for my life?
     Sir Childe, I'm not so weak;
But thinking on an absent wife
     Will blanch a faithful cheek.

7 'My spouse and boys dwell near thy hall,
     Along the bordering lake,
And when they on their father call,
     What answer shall she make?' —
'Enough, enough, my yeoman good,
     Thy grief let none gainsay;
But I, who am of lighter mood,
     Will laugh to flee away.

8 'For who would trust the seeming sighs
     Of wife or paramour?
Fresh feres will dry the bright blue eyes
     We late saw streaming o'er.
For pleasures past I do not grieve,
     Nor perils gathering near;
My greatest grief is that I leave
     No thing that claims a tear.

9 'And now I'm in the world alone,
     Upon the wide, wide sea;
But why should I for others groan,
     When none will sigh for me?
Perchance my dog will whine in vain,
     Till fed by stranger hands;
But long ere I come back again
     He'd tear me where he stands.

10　'With thee, my bark, I'll swiftly go
　　　Athwart the foaming brine;
　　Nor care what land thou bear'st me to,
　　　So not again to mine.
　　Welcome, welcome, ye dark blue waves!
　　　And when you fail my sight,
　　Welcome, ye deserts, and ye caves!
　　　My native land — Good Night!'

"Childe Harold's Pilgrimage": III, xxi–xxviii [Waterloo]

XXI　　There was a sound of revelry by night,
　　　And Belgium's capital had gather'd then
　　　Her Beauty and her Chivalry, and bright
　　　The lamps shone o'er fair women and brave men;
　　　A thousand hearts beat happily; and when
　　　Music arose with its voluptuous swell,
　　　Soft eyes look'd love to eyes which spake again,
　　　And all went merry as a marriage-bell; —
　　But hush! hark! a deep sound strikes like a rising knell!

XXII　Did ye not hear it? — No; 'twas but the wind,
　　　Or the car rattling o'er the stony street;
　　　On with the dance! let joy be unconfined;
　　　No sleep till morn, when Youth and Pleasure meet
　　　To chase the glowing Hours with flying feet —
　　　But hark! — that heavy sound breaks in once more
　　　As if the clouds its echo would repeat;
　　　And nearer, clearer, deadlier than before!
　　Arm! Arm! it is — it is — the cannon's opening roar!

XXIII　Within a window'd niche of that high hall
　　　Sate Brunswick's fated chieftain; he did hear
　　　That sound the first amidst the festival,
　　　And caught its tone with Death's prophetic ear;
　　　And when they smiled because he deem'd it near,
　　　His heart more truly knew that peal too well
　　　Which stretch'd his father on a bloody bier,
　　　And roused the vengeance blood alone could quell:
　　He rush'd into the field, and, foremost fighting, fell.

XXIV   Ah! then and there was hurrying to and fro,
           And gathering tears, and tremblings of distress,
           And cheeks all pale, which but an hour ago
           Blush'd at the praise of their own loveliness;
           And there were sudden partings, such as press
           The life from out young hearts, and choking sighs
           Which ne'er might be repeated; who could guess
           If ever more should meet those mutual eyes,
   Since upon night so sweet such awful morn could rise!

XXV   And there was mounting in hot haste: the steed,
           The mustering squadron, and the clattering car,
           Went pouring forward with impetuous speed,
           And swiftly forming in the ranks of war;
           And the deep thunder peal on peal afar;
           And near, the beat of the alarming drum
           Roused up the soldier ere the morning star;
           While throng'd the citizens with terror dumb,
   Or whispering, with white lips — 'The foe! They come! they
           come!'

XXVI   And wild and high the 'Cameron's gathering' rose!
           The war-note of Lochiel, which Albyn's hills
           Have heard, and heard too have her Saxon foes: —
           How in the noon of night that pibroch thrills,
           Savage and shrill! But with the breath which fills
           Their mountain-pipe, so fill the mountaineers
           With the fierce native daring which instils
           The stirring memory of a thousand years,
   And Evan's, Donald's fame rings in each clansman's ears!

XXVII   And Ardennes waves above them her green leaves,
           Dewy with nature's tear-drops, as they pass,
           Grieving, if aught inanimate e'er grieves,
           Over the unreturning brave, — alas!
           Ere evening to be trodden like the grass
           Which now beneath them, but above shall grow
           In its next verdure, when this fiery mass
           Of living valour, rolling on the foe
   And burning with high hope, shall moulder cold and low.

XXVIII   Last noon beheld them full of lusty life,
Last eve in Beauty's circle proudly gay,
The midnight brought the signal-sound of strife,
The morn the marshalling in arms, — the day
Battle's magnificently-stern array!
The thunder-clouds close o'er it, which when rent
The earth is cover'd thick with other clay,
Which her own clay shall cover, heap'd and pent,
Rider and horse, — friend, foe, — in one red burial blent!

"Childe Harold's Pilgrimage": IV, clxxvii–clxxxiv [Ocean]

CLXXVII   Oh that the Desert were my dwelling-place,
With one fair Spirit for my minister,
That I might all forget the human race,
And, hating no one, love but only her!
Ye Elements, in whose ennobling stir
I feel myself exalted, can ye not
Accord me such a being? Do I err
In deeming such inhabit many a spot,
Though with them to converse can rarely be our lot?

CLXXVIII   There is a pleasure in the pathless woods,
There is a rapture on the lonely shore,
There is society where none intrudes,
By the deep Sea, and music in its roar:
I love not Man the less, but Nature more,
From these our interviews, in which I steal
From all I may be or have been before,
To mingle with the Universe, and feel
What I can ne'er express, yet can not all conceal.

CLXXIX   Roll on, thou deep and dark blue Ocean, roll!
Ten thousand fleets sweep over thee in vain;
Man marks the earth with ruin, his control
Stops with the shore; upon the watery plain
The wrecks are all thy deed, nor doth remain
A shadow of man's ravage, save his own,
When, for a moment, like a drop of rain,

He sinks into thy depths with bubbling groan,
Without a grave, unknell'd, uncoffin'd, and unknown.

CLXXX   His steps are not upon thy paths, thy fields
Are not a spoil for him, — thou dost arise
And shake him from thee; the vile strength he wields
For earth's destruction thou dost all despise,
Spurning him from thy bosom to the skies,
And send'st him, shivering in thy playful spray
And howling, to his Gods, where haply lies
His petty hope in some near port or bay,
And dashest him again to earth: — there let him lay.

CLXXXI   The armaments which thunderstrike the walls
Of rock-built cities, bidding nations quake
And monarchs tremble in their capitals,
The oak leviathans, whose huge ribs make
Their clay creator the vain title take
Of lord of thee and arbiter of war, —
These are thy toys, and, as the snowy flake,
They melt into thy yeast of waves, which mar
Alike the Armada's pride or spoils of Trafalgar.

CLXXXII   Thy shores are empires, changed in all save thee —
Assyria, Greece, Rome, Carthage, what are they?
Thy waters wash'd them power while they were free,
And many a tyrant since; their shores obey
The stranger, slave, or savage; their decay
Has dried up realms to deserts: — not so thou,
Unchangeable save to thy wild waves' play;
Time writes no wrinkle on thine azure brow;
Such as creation's dawn beheld, thou rollest now.

CLXXXIII   Thou glorious mirror, where the Almighty's form
Glasses itself in tempests; in all time,
Calm or convulsed — in breeze, or gale, or storm,
Icing the pole, or in the torrid clime
Dark-heaving; — boundless, endless, and sublime —
The image of Eternity — the throne
Of the Invisible; even from out thy slime
The monsters of the deep are made; each zone
Obeys thee; thou goest forth, dread, fathomless, alone.

CLXXXIV   And I have loved thee, Ocean! and my joy
    Of youthful sports was on thy breast to be
Borne, like thy bubbles, onward. From a boy
    I wanton'd with thy breakers — they to me
Were a delight; and if the freshening sea
    Made them a terror — 'twas a pleasing fear,
For I was as it were a child of thee,
    And trusted to thy billows far and near,
And laid my hand upon thy mane — as I do here.

"Don Juan": I, cc–cciii

CC   My poem's epic, and is meant to be
    Divided in twelve books; each book containing,
With love, and war, a heavy gale at sea,
    A list of ships, and captains, and kings reigning,
New characters; the episodes are three:
    A panoramic view of hell's in training,
After the style of Virgil and of Homer,
So that my name of Epic's no misnomer.

CCI   All these things will be specified in time,
    With strict regard to Aristotle's rules,
The *Vade Mecum* of the true sublime,
    Which makes so many poets, and some fools:
Prose poets like blank-verse, I'm fond of rhyme,
    Good workmen never quarrel with their tools;
I've got new mythological machinery,
And very handsome supernatural scenery.

CCII   There's only one slight difference between
    Me and my epic brethren gone before,
And here the advantage is my own, I ween
    (Not that I have not several merits more,
But this will more peculiarly be seen);
    They so embellish, that 'tis quite a bore
Their labyrinth of fables to thread through,
Whereas this story's actually true.

CCIII   If any person doubt it, I appeal
   To history, tradition, and to facts,
  To newspapers, whose truth all know and feel,
   To plays in five, and operas in three acts;
  All these confirm my statement a good deal,
   But that which more completely faith exacts
  Is that myself, and several now in Seville,
  Saw Juan's last elopement with the devil.

"Don Juan": "The isles of Greece" (Canto III)

1 The isles of Greece, the Isles of Greece!
  Where burning Sappho loved and sung,
 Where grew the arts of war and peace,
  Where Delos rose, and Phœbus sprung!
 Eternal summer gilds them yet,
 But all, except their sun, is set.

2 The Scian and the Teian muse,*
  The hero's harp, the lover's lute,
 Have found the fame your shores refuse;
  Their place of birth alone is mute
 To sounds which echo further west
 Than your sires' 'Islands of the Blest.'

3 The mountains look on Marathon —
  And Marathon looks on the sea;
 And musing there an hour alone,
  I dream'd that Greece might still be free;
 For standing on the Persians' grave,
 I could not deem myself a slave.

---

*Homer and Anacreon.

4   A king sate on the rocky brow
         Which looks o'er sea-born Salamis;
     And ships, by thousands, lay below,
         And men in nations; — all were his!
     He counted them at break of day —
     And when the sun set where were they?

5   And where are they? and where art thou,
         My country? On thy voiceless shore
     The heroic lay is tuneless now —
         The heroic bosom beats no more!
     And must thy lyre, so long divine,
     Degenerate into hands like mine?

6   'Tis something, in the dearth of fame,
         Though link'd among a fetter'd race,
     To feel at least a patriot's shame,
         Even as I sing, suffuse my face;
     For what is left the poet here?
     For Greeks a blush — for Greece a tear.

7   Must *we* but weep o'er days more blest?
         Must *we* but blush? — Our fathers bled.
     Earth! render back from out thy breast
         A remnant of our Spartan dead!
     Of the three hundred grant but three,
     To make a new Thermopylæ!

8   What, silent still? and silent all?
         Ah! no; — the voices of the dead
     Sound like a distant torrent's fall,
         And answer, 'Let one living head,
     But one arise, — we come, we come!'
     'Tis but the living who are dumb.

9   In vain — in vain: strike other chords;
         Fill high the cup with Samian wine!
     Leave battles to the Turkish hordes,
         And shed the blood of Scio's vine!
     Hark! rising to the ignoble call —
     How answers each bold Bacchanal!

10 You have the Pyrrhic dance as yet,
        Where is the Pyrrhic phalanx gone?
    Of two such lessons, why forget
        The nobler and the manlier one?
    You have the letters Cadmus gave — *
    Think ye he meant them for a slave?

11 Fill high the bowl with Samian wine!
        We will not think of themes like these!
    It made Anacreon's song divine:
        He served — but served Polycrates —
    A tyrant; but our masters then
    Were still, at least, our countrymen.

12 The tyrant of the Chersonese
        Was freedom's best and bravest friend;
    That tyrant was Miltiades!
        Oh! that the present hour would lend
    Another despot of the kind!
    Such chains as his were sure to bind.

13 Fill high the bowl with Samian wine!
        On Suli's rock, and Parga's shore,
    Exists the remnant of a line
        Such as the Doric mothers bore;
    And there, perhaps, some seed is sown,
    The Heracleidan blood might own.

14 Trust not for freedom to the Franks —
        They have a king who buys and sells:
    In native swords, and native ranks,
        The only hope of courage dwells;
    But Turkish force, and Latin fraud,
    Would break your shield, however broad.

15 Fill high the bowl with Samian wine!
        Our virgins dance beneath the shade —
    I see their glorious black eyes shine;
        But gazing on each glowing maid,
    My own the burning tear-drop laves,
    To think such breasts must suckle slaves.

---

*Legendary creator of the Greek alphabet.

16   Place me on Sunium's marbled steep,
      Where nothing, save the waves and I,
May hear our mutual murmurs sweep;
      There, swan-like, let me sing and die:
A land of slaves shall ne'er be mine —
Dash down yon cup of Samian wine!

"Don Juan": XI, lvii–lx

LVII   Sir Walter reign'd before me; Moore and Campbell
        Before and after; but now grown more holy,
The Muses upon Sion's hill must ramble
        With poets almost clergymen, or wholly;
And Pegasus hath a psalmodic amble
        Beneath the very Reverend Rowley Powley,
Who shoes the glorious animal with stilts,
A modern Ancient Pistol — by the hilts!

LVIII   Then there's my gentle Euphues, who, they say,
        Sets up for being a sort of *moral me*;
He'll find it rather difficult some day
        To turn out both, or either, it may be.
Some persons think that Coleridge hath the sway;
        And Wordsworth has supporters, two or three;
And that deep-mouth'd Bœotian 'Savage Landor'
Has taken for a swan rogue Southey's gander.

LIX   John Keats, who was kill'd off by one critique,
        Just as he really promised something great,
If not intelligible, without Greek
        Contrived to talk about the gods of late,
Much as they might have been supposed to speak.
        Poor fellow! His was an untoward fate;
'Tis strange the mind, that very fiery particle,
Should let itself be snuff'd out by an article.

LX   The list grows long of live and dead pretenders
        To that which none will gain — or none will know
The conqueror at least; who, ere Time renders
        His last award, will have the long grass grow
Above his burnt-out brain, and sapless cinders.
        If I might augur, I should rate but low
Their chances; they're too numerous, like the thirty
Mock tyrants, when Rome's annals wax'd but dirty.

On This Day I Complete My Thirty-sixth Year

'Tis time this heart should be unmoved,
    Since others it hath ceased to move:
Yet, though I cannot be beloved,
        Still let me love!

My days are in the yellow leaf;
    The flowers and fruits of love are gone;
The worm, the canker, and the grief
        Are mine alone!

The fire that on my bosom preys
    Is lone as some volcanic isle;
No torch is kindled at its blaze —
        A funeral pile.

The hope, the fear, the jealous care,
    The exalted portion of the pain
And power of love, I cannot share,
        But wear the chain.

But 'tis not *thus* — and 'tis not *here* —
    Such thoughts should shake my soul, nor *now*,
Where glory decks the hero's bier,
        Or binds his brow.

The sword, the banner, and the field,
    Glory and Greece, around me see!
The Spartan, borne upon his shield,
        Was not more free.

Awake! (not Greece — she *is* awake!)
    Awake, my spirit! Think through *whom*
Thy life-blood tracks its parent lake,
        And then strike home!

Tread those reviving passions down,
    Unworthy manhood! — unto thee
Indifferent should the smile or frown
        Of beauty be.

If thou regret'st thy youth, *why live*?
    The land of honourable death
Is here: — up to the field, and give
        Away thy breath!

Seek out — less often sought than found —
   A soldier's grave, for thee the best;
Then look around, and choose thy ground,
      And take thy rest.

    MISSOLONGHI, *January* 22, 1824.

PERCY BYSSHE SHELLEY *(1792 – 1822)*

Hymn to Intellectual Beauty

I   The awful shadow of some unseen Power
      Floats though unseen among us, — visiting
      This various world with as inconstant wing
    As summer winds that creep from flower to flower, —
    Like moonbeams that behind some piny mountain shower,
      It visits with inconstant glance
      Each human heart and countenance;
    Like hues and harmonies of evening, —
      Like clouds in starlight widely spread, —
      Like memory of music fled, —
      Like aught that for its grace may be
    Dear, and yet dearer for its mystery.

II   Spirit of BEAUTY, that dost consecrate
      With thine own hues all thou dost shine upon
      Of human thought or form, — where art thou gone?
    Why dost thou pass away and leave our state,
    This dim vast vale of tears, vacant and desolate?
      Ask why the sunlight not for ever
      Weaves rainbows o'er yon mountain-river,
    Why aught should fail and fade that once is shown,
      Why fear and dream and death and birth
      Cast on the daylight of this earth
      Such gloom, — why man has such a scope
    For love and hate, despondency and hope?

III   No voice from some sublimer world hath ever
      To sage or poet these responses given —
      Therefore the names of Demon, Ghost, and Heaven,
    Remain the records of their vain endeavour,
    Frail spells — whose uttered charm might not avail to sever,
      From all we hear and all we see,
      Doubt, chance, and mutability.
    Thy light alone — like mist o'er mountains driven,
      Or music by the night-wind sent
      Through strings of some still instrument,
      Or moonlight on a midnight stream,
    Gives grace and truth to life's unquiet dream.

IV   Love, Hope, and Self-esteem, like clouds depart
  And come, for some uncertain moments lent.
  Man were immortal, and omnipotent,
Didst thou, unknown and awful as thou art,
Keep with thy glorious train firm state within his heart.
   Thou messenger of sympathies,
   That wax and wane in lovers' eyes —
Thou — that to human thought art nourishment,
   Like darkness to a dying flame!
   Depart not as thy shadow came,
   Depart not — lest the grave should be,
Like life and fear, a dark reality.

V   While yet a boy I sought for ghosts, and sped
  Through many a listening chamber, cave and ruin,
  And starlight wood, with fearful steps pursuing
Hopes of high talk with the departed dead.
I called on poisonous names with which our youth is fed;
   I was not heard — I saw them not —
   When musing deeply on the lot
Of life, at that sweet time when winds are wooing
   All vital things that wake to bring
   News of birds and blossoming, —
   Sudden, thy shadow fell on me;
I shrieked, and clasped my hands in ecstasy!

VI   I vowed that I would dedicate my powers
  To thee and thine — have I not kept the vow?
  With beating heart and streaming eyes, even now
I call the phantoms of a thousand hours
Each from his voiceless grave: they have in visioned bowers
   Of studious zeal or love's delight
   Outwatched with me the envious night —
They know that never joy illumed my brow
   Unlinked with hope that thou wouldst free
   This world from its dark slavery,
   That thou — O awful LOVELINESS,
Wouldst give whate'er these words cannot express.

VII   The day becomes more solemn and serene
       When noon is past — there is a harmony
      In autumn, and a lustre in its sky,
    Which through the summer is not heard or seen,
    As if it could not be, as if it had not been!
        Thus let thy power, which like the truth
        Of nature on my passive youth
    Descended, to my onward life supply
       Its calm — to one who worships thee,
       And every form containing thee,
       Whom, SPIRIT fair, thy spells did bind
    To fear himself, and love all human kind.

Ozymandias

I met a traveller from an antique land
Who said: Two vast and trunkless legs of stone
Stand in the desert . . . Near them, on the sand,
Half sunk, a shattered visage lies, whose frown,
And wrinkled lip, and sneer of cold command,
Tell that its sculptor well those passions read
Which yet survive, stamped on these lifeless things,
The hand that mocked them, and the heart that fed:
And on the pedestal these words appear:
'My name is Ozymandias, king of kings:
Look on my works, ye Mighty, and despair!'
Nothing beside remains. Round the decay
Of that colossal wreck, boundless and bare
The lone and level sands stretch far away.

Stanzas

WRITTEN IN DEJECTION, NEAR NAPLES

I   The sun is warm, the sky is clear,
     The waves are dancing fast and bright,
   Blue isles and snowy mountains wear
     The purple noon's transparent might,
     The breath of the moist earth is light,

Around its unexpanded buds;
    Like many a voice of one delight,
The winds, the birds, the ocean floods,
The City's voice itself, is soft like Solitude's.

II   I see the Deep's untrampled floor
        With green and purple seaweeds strown;
    I see the waves upon the shore,
        Like light dissolved in star-showers, thrown:
        I sit upon the sands alone, —
    The lightning of the noontide ocean
        Is flashing round me, and a tone
    Arises from its measured motion,
How sweet! did any heart now share in my emotion.

III   Alas! I have nor hope nor health,
        Nor peace within nor calm around,
    Nor that content surpassing wealth
        The sage in meditation found,
        And walked with inward glory crowned —
    Nor fame, nor power, nor love, nor leisure.
        Others I see whom these surround —
    Smiling they live, and call life pleasure; —
To me that cup has been dealt in another measure.

IV   Yet now despair itself is mild,
        Even as the winds and waters are;
    I could lie down like a tired child,
        And weep away the life of care
        Which I have borne and yet must bear,
    Till death like sleep might steal on me,
        And I might feel in the warm air
    My cheek grow cold, and hear the sea
Breathe o'er my dying brain its last monotony.

V   Some might lament that I were cold,
        As I, when this sweet day is gone,
    Which my lost heart, too soon grown old,
        Insults with this untimely moan;
        They might lament — for I am one
    Whom men love not, — and yet regret,
        Unlike this day, which, when the sun
    Shall on its stainless glory set,
Will linger, though enjoyed, like joy in memory yet.

Sonnet

Lift not the painted veil which those who live
Call Life: though unreal shapes be pictured there,
And it but mimic all we would believe
With colours idly spread, — behind, lurk Fear
And Hope, twin Destinies; who ever weave
Their shadows, o'er the chasm, sightless and drear.
I knew one who had lifted it — he sought,
For his lost heart was tender, things to love,
But found them not, alas! nor was there aught
The world contains, the which he could approve.
Through the unheeding many he did move,
A splendour among shadows, a bright blot
Upon this gloomy scene, a Spirit that strove
For truth, and like the Preacher found it not.

Song to the Men of England

I   Men of England, wherefore plough
    For the lords who lay ye low?
    Wherefore weave with toil and care
    The rich robes your tyrants wear?

II Wherefore feed, and clothe, and save,
    From the cradle to the grave,
    Those ungrateful drones who would
    Drain your sweat — nay, drink your blood?

III Wherefore, Bees of England, forge
    Many a weapon, chain, and scourge,
    That these stingless drones may spoil
    The forced produce of your toil?

IV Have ye leisure, comfort, calm,
    Shelter, food, love's gentle balm?
    Or what is it ye buy so dear
    With your pain and with your fear?

V   The seed ye sow, another reaps;
    The wealth ye find, another keeps;
    The robes ye weave, another wears;
    The arms ye forge, another bears.

VI   Sow seed, — but let no tyrant reap;
    Find wealth, — let no impostor heap;
    Weave robes, — let not the idle wear;
    Forge arms, — in your defence to bear.

VII   Shrink to your cellars, holes, and cells;
    In halls ye deck another dwells.
    Why shake the chains ye wrought? Ye see
    The steel ye tempered glance on ye.

VIII   With plough and spade, and hoe and loom,
    Trace your grave, and build your tomb,
    And weave your winding-sheet, till fair
    England be your sepulchre.

Sonnet: England in 1819

An old, mad, blind, despised, and dying king, —
Princes, the dregs of their dull race, who flow
Through public scorn, — mud from a muddy spring, —
Rulers who neither see, nor feel, nor know,
But leech-like to their fainting country cling,
Till they drop, blind in blood, without a blow, —
A people starved and stabbed in the untilled field, —
An army, which liberticide and prey
Makes as a two-edged sword to all who wield, —
Golden and sanguine laws which tempt and slay;
Religion Christless, Godless — a book sealed;
A Senate, — Time's worst statute unrepealed, —
Are graves, from which a glorious Phantom may
Burst, to illumine our tempestuous day.

Ode to the West Wind

I   O wild West Wind, thou breath of Autumn's being,
     Thou, from whose unseen presence the leaves dead
     Are driven, like ghosts from an enchanter fleeing,

     Yellow, and black, and pale, and hectic red,
     Pestilence-stricken multitudes: O thou,
     Who chariotest to their dark wintry bed

     The wingèd seeds, where they lie cold and low,
     Each like a corpse within its grave, until
     Thine azure sister of the Spring shall blow

     Her clarion o'er the dreaming earth, and fill
     (Driving sweet buds like flocks to feed in air)
     With living hues and odours plain and hill:

     Wild Spirit, which art moving everywhere;
     Destroyer and preserver; hear, oh, hear!

II   Thou on whose stream, mid the steep sky's commotion,
     Loose clouds like earth's decaying leaves are shed,
     Shook from the tangled boughs of Heaven and Ocean,

     Angels of rain and lightning: there are spread
     On the blue surface of thine aëry surge,
     Like the bright hair uplifted from the head

     Of some fierce Maenad, even from the dim verge
     Of the horizon to the zenith's height,
     The locks of the approaching storm. Thou dirge

     Of the dying year, to which this closing night
     Will be the dome of a vast sepulchre,
     Vaulted with all thy congregated might

     Of vapours, from whose solid atmosphere
     Black rain, and fire, and hail will burst: oh, hear!

III Thou who didst waken from his summer dreams
The blue Mediterranean, where he lay,
Lulled by the coil of his crystàlline streams,

Beside a pumice isle in Baiae's bay,
And saw in sleep old palaces and towers
Quivering within the wave's intenser day,

All overgrown with azure moss and flowers
So sweet, the sense faints picturing them! Thou
For whose path the Atlantic's level powers

Cleave themselves into chasms, while far below
The sea-blooms and the oozy woods which wear
The sapless foliage of the ocean, know

Thy voice, and suddenly grow gray with fear,
And tremble and despoil themselves: oh, hear!

IV If I were a dead leaf thou mightest bear;
If I were a swift cloud to fly with thee;
A wave to pant beneath thy power, and share

The impulse of thy strength, only less free
Than thou, O uncontrollable! If even
I were as in my boyhood, and could be

The comrade of thy wanderings over Heaven,
As then, when to outstrip thy skiey speed
Scarce seemed a vision; I would ne'er have striven

As thus with thee in prayer in my sore need.
Oh, lift me as a wave, a leaf, a cloud!
I fall upon the thorns of life! I bleed!

A heavy weight of hours has chained and bowed
One too like thee: tameless, and swift, and proud.

V Make me thy lyre, even as the forest is:
What if my leaves are falling like its own!
The tumult of thy mighty harmonies

Will take from both a deep, autumnal tone,
Sweet though in sadness. Be thou, Spirit fierce,
My spirit! Be thou me, impetuous one!

Drive my dead thoughts over the universe
Like withered leaves to quicken a new birth!
And, by the incantation of this verse,

Scatter, as from an unextinguished hearth
Ashes and sparks, my words among mankind!
Be through my lips to unawakened earth

The trumpet of a prophecy! O, Wind,
If Winter comes, can Spring be far behind?

The Indian Serenade

I   I arise from dreams of thee
In the first sweet sleep of night.
When the winds are breathing low,
And the stars are shining bright:
I arise from dreams of thee,
And a spirit in my feet
Hath led me — who knows how?
To thy chamber window, Sweet!

II The wandering airs they faint
On the dark, the silent stream —
The Champak odours fail
Like sweet thoughts in a dream;
The nightingale's complaint,
It dies upon her heart; —
As I must on thine,
Oh, belovèd as thou art!

III   Oh lift me from the grass!
     I die! I faint! I fail!
     Let thy love in kisses rain
     On my lips and eyelids pale.
     My cheek is cold and white, alas!
     My heart beats loud and fast; —
     Oh! press it to thine own again,
     Where it will break at last.

Love's Philosophy

I   The fountains mingle with the river
      And the rivers with the Ocean,
    The winds of Heaven mix for ever
      With a sweet emotion;
    Nothing in the world is single;
      All things by a law divine
    In one spirit meet and mingle.
      Why not I with thine? —

II   See the mountains kiss high Heaven
      And the waves clasp one another;
    No sister-flower would be forgiven
      If it disdained its brother;
    And the sunlight clasps the earth
      And the moonbeams kiss the sea:
    What is all this sweet work worth
      If thou kiss not me?

The Cloud

I bring fresh showers for the thirsting flowers,
     From the seas and the streams;
I bear light shade for the leaves when laid
     In their noonday dreams.

From my wings are shaken the dews that waken
    The sweet buds every one,
When rocked to rest on their mother's breast,
    As she dances about the sun.
I wield the flail of the lashing hail,
    And whiten the green plains under,
And then again I dissolve it in rain,
    And laugh as I pass in thunder.

I sift the snow on the mountains below,
    And their great pines groan aghast;
And all the night 'tis my pillow white,
    While I sleep in the arms of the blast.
Sublime on the towers of my skiey bowers,
    Lightning my pilot sits;
In a cavern under is fettered the thunder,
    It struggles and howls at fits;
Over earth and ocean, with gentle motion,
    This pilot is guiding me,
Lured by the love of the genii that move
    In the depths of the purple sea;
Over the rills, and the crags, and the hills,
    Over the lakes and the plains,
Wherever he dream, under mountain or stream,
    The Spirit he loves remains;
And I all the while bask in Heaven's blue smile,
    Whilst he is dissolving in rains.

The sanguine Sunrise, with his meteor eyes,
    And his burning plumes outspread,
Leaps on the back of my sailing rack,
    When the morning star shines dead;
As on the jag of a mountain crag,
    Which an earthquake rocks and swings,
An eagle alit one moment may sit
    In the light of its golden wings.
And when Sunset may breathe, from the lit sea beneath,
    Its ardours of rest and of love,
And the crimson pall of eve may fall
    From the depth of Heaven above,
With wings folded I rest, on mine aëry nest,
    As still as a brooding dove.

That orbèd maiden with white fire laden,
    Whom mortals call the Moon,
Glides glimmering o'er my fleece-like floor,
    By the midnight breezes strewn;
And wherever the beat of her unseen feet,
    Which only the angels hear,
May have broken the woof of my tent's thin roof,
    The stars peep behind her and peer;
And I laugh to see them whirl and flee,
    Like a swarm of golden bees,
When I widen the rent in my wind-built tent,
    Till the calm rivers, lakes, and seas,
Like strips of the sky fallen through me on high,
    Are each paved with the moon and these.

I bind the Sun's throne with a burning zone,
    And the Moon's with a girdle of pearl;
The volcanoes are dim, and the stars reel and swim,
    When the whirlwinds my banner unfurl.
From cape to cape, with a bridge-like shape,
    Over a torrent sea,
Sunbeam-proof, I hang like a roof, —
    The mountains its columns be.
The triumphal arch through which I march
    With hurricane, fire, and snow,
When the Powers of the air are chained to my chair,
    Is the million-coloured bow;
The sphere-fire above its soft colours wove,
    While the moist Earth was laughing below.

I am the daughter of Earth and Water,
    And the nursling of the Sky;
I pass through the pores of the ocean and shores;
    I change, but I cannot die.
For after the rain when with never a stain
    The pavilion of Heaven is bare,
And the winds and sunbeams with their convex gleams
    Build up the blue dome of air,
I silently laugh at my own cenotaph,
    And out of the caverns of rain,
Like a child from the womb, like a ghost from the tomb,
    I arise and unbuild it again.

To a Skylark

Hail to thee, blithe Spirit!
  Bird thou never wert,
That from Heaven, or near it,
  Pourest thy full heart
In profuse strains of unpremeditated art.

Higher still and higher
  From the earth thou springest
Like a cloud of fire;
  The blue deep thou wingest,
And singing still dost soar, and soaring ever singest.

In the golden lightning
  Of the sunken sun,
O'er which clouds are bright'ning,
  Thou dost float and run;
Like an unbodied joy whose race is just begun.

The pale purple even
  Melts around thy flight;
Like a star of Heaven,
  In the broad daylight
Thou art unseen, but yet I hear thy shrill delight,

Keen as are the arrows
  Of that silver sphere,
Whose intense lamp narrows
  In the white dawn clear
Until we hardly see — we feel that it is there.

All the earth and air
  With thy voice is loud,
As, when night is bare,
  From one lonely cloud
The moon rains out her beams, and Heaven is overflowed.

What thou art we know not;
  What is most like thee?
From rainbow clouds there flow not
  Drops so bright to see
As from thy presence showers a rain of melody.

Like a Poet hidden
   In the light of thought,
Singing hymns unbidden,
   Till the world is wrought
To sympathy with hopes and fears it heeded not:

Like a high-born maiden
   In a palace-tower,
Soothing her love-laden
   Soul in secret hour
With music sweet as love, which overflows her bower:

Like a glow-worm golden
   In a dell of dew,
Scattering unbeholden
   Its aëreal hue
Among the flowers and grass, which screen it from the view!

Like a rose embowered
   In its own green leaves,
By warm winds deflowered,
   Till the scent it gives
Makes faint with too much sweet those heavy-wingèd thieves:

Sound of vernal showers
   On the twinkling grass,
Rain-awakened flowers,
   All that ever was
Joyous, and clear, and fresh, thy music doth surpass:

Teach us, Sprite or Bird,
   What sweet thoughts are thine:
I have never heard
   Praise of love or wine
That panted forth a flood of rapture so divine.

Chorus Hymeneal,
   Or triumphal chant,
Matched with thine would be all
   But an empty vaunt,
A thing wherein we feel there is some hidden want.

What objects are the fountains
    Of thy happy strain?
What fields, or waves, or mountains?
    What shapes of sky or plain?
What love of thine own kind? what ignorance of pain?

With thy clear keen joyance
    Langour cannot be:
Shadow of annoyance
    Never came near thee:
Thou lovest — but ne'er knew love's sad satiety.

Waking or asleep,
    Thou of death must deem
Things more true and deep
    Than we mortals dream,
Or how could thy notes flow in such a crystal stream?

We look before and after,
    And pine for what is not:
Our sincerest laughter
    With some pain is fraught;
Our sweetest songs are those that tell of saddest thought.

Yet if we could scorn
    Hate, and pride, and fear;
If we were things born
    Not to shed a tear,
I know not how thy joy we ever should come near.

Better than all measures
    Of delightful sound,
Better than all treasures
    That in books are found,
Thy skill to poet were, thou scorner of the ground!

Teach me half the gladness
    That thy brain must know,
Such harmonious madness
    From my lips would flow
The world should listen then — as I am listening now.

Arethusa

I   Arethusa arose
      From her couch of snows
In the Acroceraunian mountains, —
      From cloud and from crag,
      With many a jag,
Shepherding her bright fountains.
      She leapt down the rocks,
      With her rainbow locks
Streaming among the streams; —
      Her steps paved with green
      The downward ravine
Which slopes to the western gleams;
      And gliding and springing
      She went, ever singing,
In murmurs as soft as sleep;
      The Earth seemed to love her,
      And Heaven smiled above her,
As she lingered towards the deep.

II   Then Alpheus bold,
      On his glacier cold,
With his trident the mountains strook;
      And opened a chasm
      In the rocks — with the spasm
All Erymanthus shook.
      And the black south wind
      It unsealed behind
The urns of the silent snow,
      And earthquake and thunder
      Did rend in sunder
The bars of the springs below.
      And the beard and the hair
      Of the River-god were
Seen through the torrent's sweep,
      As he followed the light
      Of the fleet nymph's flight
To the brink of the Dorian deep.

III   'Oh, save me! Oh, guide me!
      And bid the deep hide me,
For he grasps me now by the hair!'
      The loud Ocean heard,

To its blue depth stirred,
And divided at her prayer;
    And under the water
    The Earth's white daughter
Fled like a sunny beam;
    Behind her descended
    Her billows, unblended
With the brackish Dorian stream: —
    Like a gloomy stain
    On the emerald main
Alpheus rushed behind, —
    As an eagle pursuing
    A dove to its ruin
Down the streams of the cloudy wind.

IV   Under the bowers
    Where the Ocean Powers
Sit on their pearlèd thrones;
    Through the coral woods
    Of the weltering floods,
Over heaps of unvalued stones;
    Through the dim beams
    Which amid the streams
Weave a network of coloured light;
    And under the caves,
    Where the shadowy waves
Are as green as the forest's night: —
    Outspeeding the shark,
    And the sword-fish dark,
Under the Ocean's foam,
    And up through the rifts
    Of the mountain clifts
They passed to their Dorian home.

V   And now from their fountains
    In Enna's mountains,
Down one vale where the morning basks,
    Like friends once parted
    Grown single-hearted,
They ply their watery tasks.
    At sunrise they leap
    From their cradles steep

In the cave of the shelving hill;
   At noontide they flow
   Through the woods below
And the meadows of asphodel;
   And at night they sleep
   In the rocking deep
Beneath the Ortygian shore; —
   Like spirits that lie
   In the azure sky
When they love but live no more.

The Waning Moon

And like a dying lady, lean and pale,
Who totters forth, wrapped in a gauzy veil,
Out of her chamber, led by the insane
And feeble wanderings of her fading brain,
The moon arose up in the murky East,
A white and shapeless mass —

To the Moon

I

   Art thou pale for weariness
Of climbing heaven and gazing on the earth,
   Wandering companionless
Among the stars that have a different birth, —
And ever changing, like a joyless eye
That finds no object worth its constancy?

II

   Thou chosen sister of the Spirit,
That gazes on thee till in thee it pities . . .

To Night

I   Swiftly walk o'er the western wave,
        Spirit of Night!
Out of the misty eastern cave,
Where, all the long and lone daylight,
Thou wovest dreams of joy and fear,
Which make thee terrible and dear, —
        Swift be thy flight!

II   Wrap thy form in a mantle gray,
        Star-inwrought!
Blind with thine hair the eyes of Day;
Kiss her until she be wearied out,
Then wander o'er city, and sea, and land,
Touching all with thine opiate wand —
        Come, long-sought!

III   When I arose and saw the dawn,
        I sighed for thee;
When light rode high, and the dew was gone,
And noon lay heavy on flower and tree,
And the weary Day turned to his rest,
Lingering like an unloved guest,
        I sighed for thee.

IV   Thy brother Death came, and cried,
        Wouldst thou me?
Thy sweet child Sleep, the filmy-eyed,
Murmured like a noontide bee,
Shall I nestle near thy side?
Wouldst thou me? — And I replied,
        No, not thee!

V   Death will come when thou art dead,
        Soon, too soon —
Sleep will come when thou art fled;
Of neither would I ask the boon
I ask of thee, belovèd Night —
Swift be thine approaching flight,
        Come soon, soon!

To ——

Music, when soft voices die,
Vibrates in the memory —
Odours, when sweet violets sicken,
Live within the sense they quicken.

Rose leaves, when the rose is dead,
Are heaped for the belovèd's bed;
And so thy thoughts, when thou art gone,
Love itself shall slumber on.

Song

I   Rarely, rarely, comest thou,
         Spirit of Delight!
     Wherefore hast thou left me now
         Many a day and night?
     Many a weary night and day
     'Tis since thou art fled away.

II   How shall ever one like me
         Win thee back again?
     With the joyous and the free
         Thou wilt scoff at pain.
     Spirit false! thou hast forgot
         All but those who need thee not.

III As a lizard with the shade
         Of a trembling leaf,
     Thou with sorrow art dismayed;
         Even the sighs of grief
     Reproach thee, that thou art not near,
     And reproach thou wilt not hear.

IV   Let me set my mournful ditty
         To a merry measure;
     Thou wilt never come for pity,
         Thou wilt come for pleasure;
     Pity then will cut away
     Those cruel wings, and thou wilt stay.

V   I love all that thou lovest,
       Spirit of Delight!
     The fresh Earth in new leaves dressed,
       And the starry night;
     Autumn evening, and the morn
     When the golden mists are born.

VI   I love snow, and all the forms
       Of the radiant frost;
     I love waves, and winds, and storms,
       Everything almost
     Which is Nature's, and may be
     Untainted by man's misery.

VII   I love tranquil solitude,
       And such society
     As is quiet, wise, and good;
       Between thee and me
     What difference? but thou dost possess
     The things I seek, not love them less.

VIII I love Love — though he has wings,
       And like light can flee,
     But above all other things,
       Spirit, I love thee —
     Thou art love and life! Oh, come,
     Make once more my heart thy home.

Adonais

AN ELEGY ON THE DEATH OF JOHN KEATS, AUTHOR OF ENDYMION, HYPERION, ETC.

Ἀστὴρ πρὶν μὲν ἔλαμπες ἐνὶ ζωοῖσιν Ἑῷος.
νῦν δὲ θανὼν λάμπεις Ἕσπερος ἐν φθιμένοις. — Plato*

I   I weep for Adonais — he is dead!
       O, weep for Adonais! though our tears
       Thaw not the frost which binds so dear a head!

---

*Formerly you shone among the living like the star of dawn; now, dead, you shine like the evening star among the departed.

And thou, sad Hour, selected from all years
To mourn our loss, rouse thy obscure compeers,
And teach them thine own sorrow, say: 'With me
Died Adonais; till the Future dares
Forget the Past, his fate and fame shall be
An echo and a light unto eternity!'

II   Where wert thou, mighty Mother, when he lay,
When thy Son lay, pierced by the shaft which flies
In darkness? where was lorn Urania
When Adonais died? With veilèd eyes,
'Mid listening Echoes, in her Paradise
She sate, while one, with soft enamoured breath,
Rekindled all the fading melodies,
With which, like flowers that mock the corse beneath,
He had adorned and hid the coming bulk of Death.

III   Oh, weep for Adonais — he is dead!
Wake, melancholy Mother, wake and weep!
Yet wherefore? Quench within their burning bed
Thy fiery tears, and let thy loud heart keep
Like his, a mute and uncomplaining sleep;
For he is gone, where all things wise and fair
Descend; — oh, dream not that the amorous Deep
Will yet restore him to the vital air;
Death feeds on his mute voice, and laughs at our despair.

IV   Most musical of mourners, weep again!
Lament anew, Urania! — He died,
Who was the Sire of an immortal strain,
Blind, old, and lonely, when his country's pride,
The priest, the slave, and the liberticide,
Trampled and mocked with many a loathèd rite
Of lust and blood; he went, unterrified,
Into the gulf of death; but his clear Sprite
Yet reigns o'er earth; the third among the sons of light.

V   Most musical of mourners, weep anew!
Not all to that bright station dared to climb;
And happier they their happiness who knew,
Whose tapers yet burn through that night of time
In which suns perished; others more sublime,
Struck by the envious wrath of man or god,

Have sunk, extinct in their refulgent prime;
And some yet live, treading the thorny road,
Which leads, through toil and hate, to Fame's serene abode.

VI   But now, thy youngest, dearest one, has perished —
The nursling of thy widowhood, who grew,
Like a pale flower by some sad maiden cherished,
And fed with true-love tears, instead of dew;
Most musical of mourners, weep anew!
Thy extreme hope, the loveliest and the last,
The bloom, whose petals nipped before they blew
Died on the promise of the fruit, is waste;
The broken lily lies — the storm is overpast.

VII   To that high Capital, where kingly Death
Keeps his pale court in beauty and decay,
He came; and bought, with price of purest breath,
A grave among the eternal. — Come away!
Haste, while the vault of blue Italian day
Is yet his fitting charnel-roof! while still
He lies, as if in dewy sleep he lay;
Awake him not! surely he takes his fill
Of deep and liquid rest, forgetful of all ill.

VIII   He will awake no more, oh, never more! —
Within the twilight chamber spreads apace
The shadow of white Death, and at the door
Invisible Corruption waits to trace
His extreme way to her dim dwelling-place;
The eternal Hunger sits, but pity and awe
Soothe her pale rage, nor dares she to deface
So fair a prey, till darkness, and the law
Of change, shall o'er his sleep the mortal curtain draw.

IX   Oh, weep for Adonais! — The quick Dreams,
The passion-wingèd Ministers of thought,
Who were his flocks, whom near the living streams
Of his young spirit he fed, and whom he taught
The love which was its music, wander not, —
Wander no more, from kindling brain to brain,
But droop there, whence they sprung; and mourn their lot
Round the cold heart, where, after their sweet pain,
They ne'er will gather strength, or find a home again.

X   And one with trembling hands clasps his cold head,
        And fans him with her moonlight wings, and cries;
        'Our love, our hope, our sorrow, is not dead;
        See, on the silken fringe of his faint eyes,
        Like dew upon a sleeping flower, there lies
        A tear some Dream has loosened from his brain.'
        Lost Angel of a ruined Paradise!
        She knew not 'twas her own; as with no stain
    She faded, like a cloud which had outwept its rain.

XI   One from a lucid urn of starry dew
        Washed his light limbs as if embalming them;
        Another clipped her profuse locks, and threw
        The wreath upon him, like an anadem,
        Which frozen tears instead of pearls begem;
        Another in her wilful grief would break
        Her bow and wingèd reeds, as if to stem
        A greater loss with one which was more weak;
    And dull the barbèd fire against his frozen cheek.

XII   Another Splendour on his mouth alit,
        That mouth, whence it was wont to draw the breath
        Which gave it strength to pierce the guarded wit,
        And pass into the panting heart beneath
        With lightning and with music: the damp death
        Quenched its caress upon his icy lips;
        And, as a dying meteor stains a wreath
        Of moonlight vapour, which the cold night clips,
    It flushed through his pale limbs, and passed to its eclipse.

XIII   And others came . . . Desires and Adorations,
        Wingèd Persuasions and veiled Destinies,
        Splendours, and Glooms, and glimmering Incarnations
        Of hopes and fears, and twilight Phantasies;
        And Sorrow, with her family of Sighs,
        And Pleasure, blind with tears, led by the gleam
        Of her own dying smile instead of eyes,
        Came in slow pomp; — the moving pomp might seem
    Like pageantry of mist on an autumnal stream.

XIV All he had loved, and moulded into thought,
     From shape, and hue, and odour, and sweet sound,
     Lamented Adonais. Morning sought
     Her eastern watch-tower, and her hair unbound,
     Wet with the tears which should adorn the ground,
     Dimmed the aëreal eyes that kindle day;
     Afar the melancholy thunder moaned,
     Pale Ocean in unquiet slumber lay,
And the wild Winds flew round, sobbing in their dismay.

XV   Lost Echo sits amid the voiceless mountains,
     And feeds her grief with his remembered lay,
     And will no more reply to winds or fountains,
     Or amorous birds perched on the young green spray,
     Or herdsman's horn, or bell at closing day;
     Since she can mimic not his lips, more dear
     Than those for whose disdain she pined away
     Into a shadow of all sounds: — a drear
Murmur, between their songs, is all the woodmen hear.

XVI Grief made the young Spring wild, and she threw down
     Her kindling buds, as if she Autumn were,
     Or they dead leaves; since her delight is flown,
     For whom should she have waked the sullen year?
     To Phoebus was not Hyacinth so dear
     Nor to himself Narcissus, as to both
     Thou, Adonais: wan they stand and sere
     Amid the faint companions of their youth,
With dew all turned to tears; odour, to sighing ruth.

XVII Thy spirit's sister, the lorn nightingale
     Mourns not her mate with such melodious pain;
     Not so the eagle, who like thee could scale
     Heaven, and could nourish in the sun's domain
     Her mighty youth with morning, doth complain,
     Soaring and screaming round her empty nest,
     As Albion wails for thee: the curse of Cain
     Light on his head who pierced thy innocent breast,
And scared the angel soul that was its earthly guest!

XVIII Ah, woe is me! Winter is come and gone,
    But grief returns with the revolving year;
    The airs and streams renew their joyous tone;
    The ants, the bees, the swallows reappear;
    Fresh leaves and flowers deck the dead Seasons' bier;
    The amorous birds now pair in every brake,
    And build their mossy homes in field and brere;
    And the green lizard, and the golden snake,
Like unimprisoned flames, out of their trance awake.

XIX Through wood and stream and field and hill and Ocean
    A quickening life from the Earth's heart has burst
    As it has ever done, with change and motion,
    From the great morning of the world when first
    God dawned on Chaos; in its stream immersed,
    The lamps of Heaven flash with a softer light;
    All baser things pant with life's sacred thirst;
    Diffuse themselves; and spend in love's delight,
The beauty and the joy of their renewèd might.

XX The leprous corpse, touched by this spirit tender,
    Exhales itself in flowers of gentle breath;
    Like incarnations of the stars, when splendour
    Is changed to fragrance, they illumine death
    And mock the merry worm that wakes beneath;
    Nought we know, dies. Shall that alone which knows
    Be as a sword consumed before the sheath
    By sightless lightning? — the intense atom glows
A moment, then is quenched in a most cold repose.

XXI Alas! that all we loved of him should be,
    But for our grief, as if it had not been,
    And grief itself be mortal! Woe is me!
    Whence are we, and why are we? of what scene
    The actors or spectators? Great and mean
    Meet massed in death, who lends what life must borrow.
    As long as skies are blue, and fields are green,
    Evening must usher night, night urge the morrow,
Month follow month with woe, and year wake year to sorrow.

XXII   *He* will awake no more, oh, never more!
         'Wake thou,' cried Misery, 'childless Mother, rise
         Out of thy sleep, and slake, in thy heart's core,
         A wound more fierce than his, with tears and sighs.'
         And all the Dreams that watched Urania's eyes,
         And all the Echoes whom their sister's song
         Had held in holy silence, cried: 'Arise!'
         Swift as a Thought by the snake Memory stung,
     From her ambrosial rest the fading Splendour sprung.

XXIII   She rose like an autumnal Night, that springs
         Out of the East, and follows wild and drear
         The golden Day, which, on eternal wings,
         Even as a ghost abandoning a bier,
         Had left the Earth a corpse. Sorrow and fear
         So struck, so roused, so rapt Urania;
         So saddened round her like an atmosphere
         Of stormy mist; so swept her on her way
     Even to the mournful place where Adonais lay.

XXIV   Out of her secret Paradise she sped,
         Through camps and cities rough with stone, and steel,
         And human hearts, which to her aery tread
         Yielding not, wounded the invisible
         Palms of her tender feet where'er they fell:
         And barbèd tongues, and thoughts more sharp than they,
         Rent the soft Form they never could repel,
         Whose sacred blood, like the young tears of May,
     Paved with eternal flowers that undeserving way.

XXV   In the death-chamber for a moment Death,
         Shamed by the presence of that living Might,
         Blushed to annihilation, and the breath
         Revisited those lips, and Life's pale light
         Flashed through those limbs, so late her dear delight.
         'Leave me not wild and drear and comfortless,
         As silent lightning leaves the starless night!
         Leave me not!' cried Urania: her distress
     Roused Death: Death rose and smiled, and met her vain caress.

XXVI   'Stay yet awhile! speak to me once again;
         Kiss me, so long but as a kiss may live;
         And in my heartless breast and burning brain
         That word, that kiss, shall all thoughts else survive,
         With food of saddest memory kept alive,
         Now thou art dead, as if it were a part
         Of thee, my Adonais! I would give
         All that I am to be as thou now art!
But I am chained to Time, and cannot thence depart!

XXVII   'O gentle child, beautiful as thou wert,
         Why didst thou leave the trodden paths of men
         Too soon, and with weak hands though mighty heart
         Dare the unpastured dragon in his den?
         Defenceless as thou wert, oh, where was then
         Wisdom the mirrored shield, or scorn the spear?
         Or hadst thou waited the full cycle, when
         Thy spirit should have filled its crescent sphere,
The monsters of life's waste had fled from thee like deer.

XXVIII   'The herded wolves, bold only to pursue;
         The obscene ravens, clamorous o'er the dead;
         The vultures to the conqueror's banner true
         Who feed where Desolation first has fed,
         And whose wings rain contagion; — how they fled,
         When, like Apollo, from his golden bow
         The Pythian of the age one arrow sped
         And smiled! — The spoilers tempt no second blow,
They fawn on the proud feet that spurn them lying low.

XXIX   'The sun comes forth, and many reptiles spawn;
         He sets, and each ephemeral insect then
         Is gathered into death without a dawn,
         And the immortal stars awake again;
         So is it in the world of living men:
         A godlike mind soars forth, in its delight
         Making earth bare and veiling heaven, and when
         It sinks, the swarms that dimmed or shared its light
Leave to its kindred lamps the spirit's awful night.'

XXX   Thus ceased she: and the mountain shepherds came,
       Their garlands sere, their magic mantles rent;
       The Pilgrim of Eternity, whose fame
       Over his living head like Heaven is bent,
       An early but enduring monument,
       Came, veiling all the lightnings of his song
       In sorrow; from her wilds Ierne sent
       The sweetest lyrist of her saddest wrong,
    And Love taught Grief to fall like music from his tongue.

XXXI   Midst others of less note, came one frail Form,
       A phantom among men; companionless
       As the last cloud of an expiring storm
       Whose thunder is its knell; he, as I guess,
       Had gazed on Nature's naked loveliness,
       Actaeon-like, and now he fled astray
       With feeble steps o'er the world's wilderness,
       And his own thoughts, along that rugged way,
    Pursued, like raging hounds, their father and their prey.

XXXII A pardlike Spirit beautiful and swift —
       A Love in desolation masked; — a Power
       Girt round with weakness; — it can scarce uplift
       The weight of the superincumbent hour;
       It is a dying lamp, a falling shower,
       A breaking billow; — even whilst we speak
       Is it not broken? On the withering flower
       The killing sun smiles brightly: on a cheek
    The life can burn in blood, even while the heart may break.

XXXIII His head was bound with pansies overblown,
       And faded violets, white, and pied, and blue;
       And a light spear topped with a cypress cone,
       Round whose rude shaft dark ivy-tresses grew
       Yet dripping with the forest's noonday dew,
       Vibrated, as the ever-beating heart
       Shook the weak hand that grasped it; of that crew
       He came the last, neglected and apart;
    A herd-abandoned deer struck by the hunter's dart.

XXXIV   All stood aloof, and at his partial moan
           Smiled through their tears; well knew that gentle band
           Who in another's fate now wept his own,
           As in the accents of an unknown land
           He sung new sorrow; sad Urania scanned
           The Stranger's mien, and murmured: 'Who art thou?'
           He answered not, but with a sudden hand
           Made bare his branded and ensanguined brow,
    Which was like Cain's or Christ's — oh! that it should be so!

XXXV   What softer voice is hushed over the dead?
           Athwart what brow is that dark mantle thrown?
           What form leans sadly o'er the white death-bed,
           In mockery of monumental stone,
           The heavy heart heaving without a moan?
           If it be He, who, gentlest of the wise,
           Taught, soothed, loved, honoured the departed one,
           Let me not vex, with inharmonious sighs,
    The silence of that heart's accepted sacrifice.

XXXVI   Our Adonais has drunk poison — oh!
           What deaf and viperous murderer could crown
           Life's early cup with such a draught of woe?
           The nameless worm would now itself disown:
           It felt, yet could escape, the magic tone
           Whose prelude held all envy, hate, and wrong,
           But what was howling in one breast alone,
           Silent with expectation of the song,
    Whose master's hand is cold, whose silver lyre unstrung.

XXXVII   Live thou, whose infamy is not thy fame!
           Live! fear no heavier chastisement from me,
           Thou noteless blot on a remembered name!
           But be thyself, and know thyself to be!
           And ever at thy season be thou free
           To spill the venom when thy fangs o'erflow;
           Remorse and Self-contempt shall cling to thee;
           Hot Shame shall burn upon thy secret brow,
    And like a beaten hound tremble thou shalt — as now.

XXXVIII   Nor let us weep that our delight is fled
            Far from these carrion kites that scream below;
            He wakes or sleeps with the enduring dead;
            Thou canst nor soar where he is sitting now. —
            Dust to the dust! but the pure spirit shall flow
            Back to the burning fountain whence it came,
            A portion of the Eternal, which must glow
            Through time and change, unquenchably the same,
        Whilst thy cold embers choke the sordid hearth of shame.

XXXIX   Peace, peace! he is not dead, he doth not sleep —
            He hath awakened from the dream of life —
            'Tis we, who lost in stormy visions, keep
            With phantoms an unprofitable strife,
            And in mad trance, strike with our spirit's knife
            Invulnerable nothings. — We decay
            Like corpses in a charnel; fear and grief
            Convulse us and consume us day by day,
        And cold hopes swarm like worms within our living clay.

XL   He has outsoared the shadow of our night;
            Envy and calumny and hate and pain,
            And that unrest which men miscall delight,
            Can touch him not and torture not again;
            From the contagion of the world's slow stain
            He is secure, and now can never mourn
            A heart grown cold, a head grown gray in vain;
            Nor, when the spirit's self has ceased to burn,
        With sparkless ashes load an unlamented urn.

XLI   He lives, he wakes — 'tis Death is dead, not he;
            Mourn not for Adonais. — Thou young Dawn,
            Turn all thy dew to splendour, for from thee
            The spirit thou lamentest is not gone;
            Ye caverns and ye forests, cease to moan!
            Cease, ye faint flowers and fountains, and thou Air,
            Which like a mourning veil thy scarf hadst thrown
            O'er the abandoned Earth, now leave it bare
        Even to the joyous stars which smile on its despair!

XLII   He is made one with Nature: there is heard
        His voice in all her music, from the moan
        Of thunder, to the song of night's sweet bird;
        He is a presence to be felt and known
        In darkness and in light, from herb and stone,
        Spreading itself where'er that Power may move
        Which has withdrawn his being to its own;
        Which wields the world with never-wearied love,
Sustains it from beneath, and kindles it above.

XLIII   He is a portion of the loveliness
        Which once he made more lovely: he doth bear
        His part, while the one Spirit's plastic stress
        Sweeps through the dull dense world, compelling there,
        All new successions to the forms they wear;
        Torturing th' unwilling dross that checks its flight
        To its own likeness, as each mass may bear;
        And bursting in its beauty and its might
From trees and beasts and men into the Heaven's light.

XLIV   The splendours of the firmament of time
        May be eclipsed, but are extinguished not;
        Like stars to their appointed height they climb,
        And death is a low mist which cannot blot
        The brightness it may veil. When lofty thought
        Lifts a young heart above its mortal lair,
        And love and life contend in it, for what
        Shall be its earthly doom, the dead live there
And move like winds of light on dark and stormy air.

XLV   The inheritors of unfulfilled renown
        Rose from their thrones, built beyond mortal thought,
        Far in the Unapparent. Chatterton
        Rose pale, — his solemn agony had not
        Yet faded from him; Sidney, as he fought
        And as he fell and as he lived and loved
        Sublimely mild, a Spirit without spot,
        Arose; and Lucan, by his death approved:
Oblivion as they rose shrank like a thing reproved.

XLVI   And many more, whose names on Earth are dark,
          But whose transmitted effluence cannot die
          So long as fire outlives the parent spark,
          Rose, robed in dazzling immortality.
          'Thou art become as one of us,' they cry,
          'It was for thee yon kingless sphere has long
          Swung blind in unascended majesty,
          Silent alone amid an Heaven of Song.
    Assume thy wingèd throne, thou Vesper of our throng!'

XLVII   Who mourns for Adonais? Oh, come forth,
          Fond wretch! and know thyself and him aright.
          Clasp with thy panting soul the pendulous Earth;
          As from a centre, dart thy spirit's light
          Beyond all worlds, until its spacious might
          Satiate the void circumference: then shrink
          Even to a point within our day and night;
          And keep thy heart light lest it make thee sink
    When hope has kindled hope, and lured thee to the brink.

XLVIII   Or go to Rome, which is the sepulchre,
          Oh, not of him, but of our joy: 'tis nought
          That ages, empires, and religions there
          Lie buried in the ravage they have wrought;
          For such as he can lend, — they borrow not
          Glory from those who made the world their prey;
          And he is gathered to the kings of thought
          Who waged contention with their time's decay,
    And of the past are all that cannot pass away.

XLIX   Go thou to Rome, — at once the Paradise,
          The grave, the city, and the wilderness;
          And where its wrecks like shattered mountains rise,
          And flowering weeds, and fragrant copses dress
          The bones of Desolation's nakedness
          Pass, till the spirit of the spot shall lead
          Thy footsteps to a slope of green access
          Where, like an infant's smile, over the dead
    A light of laughing flowers along the grass is spread;

L   And gray walls moulder round, on which dull Time
           Feeds, like slow fire upon a hoary brand;
           And one keen pyramid with wedge sublime,
           Pavilioning the dust of him who planned
           This refuge for his memory, doth stand
           Like flame transformed to marble; and beneath,
           A field is spread, on which a newer band
           Have pitched in Heaven's smile their camp of death,
    Welcoming him we lose with scarce extinguished breath.

LI   Here pause: these graves are all too young as yet
           To have outgrown the sorrow which consigned
           Its charge to each; and if the seal is set,
           Here, on one fountain of a mourning mind,
           Break it not thou! too surely shalt thou find
           Thine own well full, if thou returnest home,
           Of tears and gall. From the world's bitter wind
           Seek shelter in the shadow of the tomb.
    What Adonais is, why fear we to become?

LII   The One remains, the many change and pass;
           Heaven's light forever shines, Earth's shadows fly;
           Life, like a dome of many-coloured glass,
           Stains the white radiance of Eternity,
           Until Death tramples it to fragments. — Die,
           If thou wouldst be with that which thou dost seek!
           Follow where all is fled! — Rome's azure sky,
           Flowers, ruins, statues, music, words, are weak
    The glory they transfuse with fitting truth to speak.

LIII   Why linger, why turn back, why shrink, my Heart?
           Thy hopes are gone before: from all things here
           They have departed; thou shouldst now depart!
           A light is passed from the revolving year,
           And man, and woman; and what still is dear
           Attracts to crush, repels to make thee wither.
           The soft sky smiles, — the low wind whispers near:
           'Tis Adonais calls! oh, hasten thither,
    No more let Life divide what Death can join together.

LIV That Light whose smile kindles the Universe,
    That Beauty in which all things work and move,
    That Benediction which the eclipsing Curse
    Of birth can quench not, that sustaining Love
    Which through the web of being blindly wove
    By man and beast and earth and air and sea,
    Burns bright or dim, as each are mirrors of
    The fire for which all thirst; now beams on me,
  Consuming the last clouds of cold mortality.

LV The breath whose might I have invoked in song
    Descends on me; my spirit's bark is driven,
    Far from the shore, far from the trembling throng
    Whose sails were never to the tempest given;
    The massy earth and spherèd skies are riven!
    I am borne darkly, fearfully, afar;
    Whilst, burning through the inmost veil of Heaven,
    The soul of Adonais, like a star,
  Beacons from the abode where the Eternal are.

Hellas

A LYRICAL DRAMA

Final Chorus

The world's great age begins anew,
 The golden years return,
The earth doth like a snake renew
 Her winter weeds outworn:
Heaven smiles, and faiths and empires gleam,
Like wrecks of a dissolving dream.

A brighter Hellas rears its mountains
 From waves serener far;
A new Peneus rolls his fountains
 Against the morning star.
Where fairer Tempes bloom, there sleep
Young Cyclads on a sunnier deep.

A loftier Argo cleaves the main,
    Fraught with a later prize;
Another Orpheus sings again,
    And loves, and weeps, and dies.
A new Ulysses leaves once more
Calypso for his native shore.

Oh, write no more the tale of Troy,
    If earth Death's scroll must be!
Nor mix with Laian rage the joy
    Which dawns upon the free:
Although a subtler Sphinx renew
Riddles of death Thebes never knew.

Another Athens shall arise,
    And to remoter time
Bequeath, like sunset to the skies,
    The splendour of its prime;
And leave, if nought so bright may live,
All earth can take or Heaven can give.

Saturn and Love their long repose
    Shall burst, more bright and good
Than all who fell, than One who rose,
    Than many unsubdued:
Not gold, not blood, their altar dowers,
But votive tears and symbol flowers.

Oh, cease! must hate and death return?
    Cease! must men kill and die?
Cease! drain not to its dregs the urn
    Of bitter prophecy.
The world is weary of the past,
Oh, might it die or rest at last!

Lines: "When the Lamp Is Shattered"

I   When the lamp is shattered
    The light in the dust lies dead —
       When the cloud is scattered
    The rainbow's glory is shed.

     When the lute is broken,
Sweet tones are remembered not;
     When the lips have spoken,
Loved accents are soon forgot.

II   As music and splendour
Survive not the lamp and the lute,
     The heart's echoes render
No song when the spirit is mute: —
     No song but sad dirges,
Like the wind through a ruined cell,
     Or the mournful surges
That ring the dead seaman's knell.

III   When hearts have once mingled
Love first leaves the well-built nest;
     The weak one is singled
To endure what it once possessed.
     O Love! who bewailest
The frailty of all things here,
     Why choose you the frailest
For your cradle, your home, and your bier?

IV   Its passions will rock thee
As the storms rock the ravens on high;
     Bright reason will mock thee,
Like the sun from a wintry sky.
     From thy nest every rafter
Will rot, and thine eagle home
     Leave thee naked to laughter,
When leaves fall and cold winds come.

To Jane: The Invitation

Best and brightest, come away!
Fairer far than this fair Day,
Which, like thee to those in sorrow,
Comes to bid a sweet good-morrow
To the rough Year just awake
In its cradle on the brake.

The brightest hour of unborn Spring,
Through the winter wandering,
Found, it seems, the halcyon Morn
To hoar February born.
Bending from Heaven, in azure mirth,
It kissed the forehead of the Earth,
And smiled upon the silent sea,
And bade the frozen streams be free,
And waked to music all their fountains,
And breathed upon the frozen mountains,
And like a prophetess of May
Strewed flowers upon the barren way,
Making the wintry world appear
Like one on whom thou smilest, dear.

Away, away, from men and towns,
To the wild wood and the downs —
To the silent wilderness
Where the soul need not repress
Its music lest it should not find
An echo in another's mind,
While the touch of Nature's art
Harmonizes heart to heart.
I leave this notice on my door
For each accustomed visitor: —
'I am gone into the fields
To take what this sweet hour yields; —
Reflection, you may come to-morrow,
Sit by the fireside with Sorrow. —
You with the unpaid bill, Despair, —
You, tiresome verse-reciter, Care, —
I will pay you in the grave, —
Death will listen to your stave.
Expectation too, be off!
To-day is for itself enough;
Hope, in pity mock not Woe
With smiles, nor follow where I go;
Long having lived on thy sweet food,
At length I find one moment's good
After long pain — with all your love,
This you never told me of.'

Radiant Sister of the Day,
Awake! arise! and come away!
To the wild woods and the plains,
And the pools where winter rains
Image all their roof of leaves,
Where the pine its garland weaves
Of sapless green and ivy dun
Round stems that never kiss the sun;
Where the lawns and pastures be,
And the sandhills of the sea; —
Where the melting hoar-frost wets
The daisy-star that never sets,
And wind-flowers, and violets,
Which yet join not scent to hue,
Crown the pale year weak and new;
When the night is left behind
In the deep east, dun and blind,
And the blue noon is over us,
And the multitudinous
Billows murmur at our feet,
Where the earth and ocean meet,
And all things seem only one
In the universal sun.

To Jane: The Recollection

I   Now the last day of many days,
        All beautiful and bright as thou,
            The loveliest and the last, is dead,
    Rise, Memory, and write its praise!
        Up, — to thy wonted work! come, trace
            The epitaph of glory fled, —
    For now the Earth has changed its face,
        A frown is on the Heaven's brow.

II We wandered to the Pine Forest
        That skirts the Ocean's foam,
    The lightest wind was in its nest,
        The tempest in its home.
    The whispering waves were half asleep,
        The clouds were gone to play,

And on the bosom of the deep
  The smile of Heaven lay;
It seemed as if the hour were one
  Sent from beyond the skies,
Which scattered from above the sun
  A light of Paradise.

III   We paused amid the pines that stood
      The giants of the waste,
  Tortured by storms to shapes as rude
      As serpents interlaced,
  And soothed by every azure breath,
      That under Heaven is blown,
  To harmonies and hues beneath,
      As tender as its own;
  Now all the tree-tops lay asleep,
      Like green waves on the sea,
  As still as in the silent deep
      The ocean woods may be.

IV   How calm it was! — the silence there
      By such a chain was bound
  That even the busy woodpecker
      Made stiller by her sound
  The inviolable quietness;
      The breath of peace we drew
  With its soft motion made not less
      The calm that round us grew.
  There seemed from the remotest seat
      Of the white mountain waste,
  To the soft flower beneath our feet,
      A magic circle traced, —
  A spirit interfused around,
      A thrilling, silent life, —
  To momentary peace it bound
      Our mortal nature's strife;
  And still I felt the centre of
      The magic circle there
  Was one fair form that filled with love
      The lifeless atmosphere.

V We paused beside the pools that lie
       Under the forest bough, —
   Each seemed as 'twere a little sky
       Gulfed in a world below;
   A firmament of purple light
       Which in the dark earth lay,
   More boundless than the depth of night,
       And purer than the day —
   In which the lovely forests grew,
       As in the upper air,
   More perfect both in shape and hue
       Than any spreading there.
   There lay the glade and neighbouring lawn,
       And through the dark green wood
         The white sun twinkling like the dawn
       Out of a speckled cloud.
   Sweet views which in our world above
       Can never well be seen,
   Were imaged by the water's love
       Of that fair forest green.
   And all was interfused beneath
       With an Elysian glow,
   An atmosphere without a breath,
       A softer day below.
   Like one beloved the scene had lent
       To the dark water's breast,
   Its every leaf and lineament
       With more than truth expressed;
   Until an envious wind crept by,
       Like an unwelcome thought,
   Which from the mind's too faithful eye
       Blots one dear image out.
   Though thou art ever fair and kind,
       The forests ever green,
   Less oft is peace in Shelley's mind,
       Than calm in waters, seen.

With a Guitar, to Jane

Ariel to Miranda: — Take
This slave of Music, for the sake
Of him who is the slave of thee,
And teach it all the harmony
In which thou canst, and only thou,
Make the delighted spirit glow,
Till joy denies itself again,
And, too intense, is turned to pain;
For by permission and command
Of thine own Prince Ferdinand,
Poor Ariel sends this silent token
Of more than ever can be spoken;
Your guardian spirit, Ariel, who,
From life to life, must still pursue
Your happiness; — for thus alone
Can Ariel ever find his own.
From Prospero's enchanted cell,
As the mighty verses tell,
To the throne of Naples, he
Lit you o'er the trackless sea,
Flitting on, your prow before,
Like a living meteor.
When you die, the silent Moon,
In her interlunar swoon,
Is not sadder in her cell
Than deserted Ariel.
When you live again on earth,
Like an unseen star of birth,
Ariel guides you o'er the sea
Of life from your nativity.
Many changes have been run
Since Ferdinand and you begun
Your course of love, and Ariel still
Has tracked your steps, and served your will;
Now, in humbler, happier lot,
This is all remembered not;
And now, alas! the poor sprite is
Imprisoned, for some fault of his,
In a body like a grave; —

From you he only dares to crave,
For his service and his sorrow,
A smile to-day, a song to-morrow.
The artist who this idol wrought,
To echo all harmonious thought,
Felled a tree, while on the steep
The woods were in their winter sleep,
Rocked in that repose divine
On the wind-swept Apennine;
And dreaming, some of Autumn past,
And some of Spring approaching fast,
And some of April buds and showers,
And some of songs in July bowers,
And all of love; and so this tree, —
O that such our death may be! —
Died in sleep, and felt no pain,
To live in happier form again:
From which, beneath Heaven's fairest star,
The artist wrought this loved Guitar,
And taught it justly to reply,
To all who question skilfully,
In language gentle as thine own;
Whispering in enamoured tone
Sweet oracles of woods and dells,
And summer winds in sylvan cells;
For it had learned all harmonies
Of the plains and of the skies,
Of the forests and the mountains,
And the many-voicèd fountains;
The clearest echoes of the hills,
The softest notes of falling rills,
The melodies of birds and bees,
The murmuring of summer seas,
And pattering rain, and breathing dew,
And airs of evening; and it knew
That seldom-heard mysterious sound,
Which, driven on its diurnal round,
As it floats through boundless day,
Our world enkindles on its way. —
All this it knows, but will not tell
To those who cannot question well
The Spirit that inhabits it;

It talks according to the wit
Of its companions; and no more
Is heard than has been felt before,
By those who tempt it to betray
These secrets of an elder day:
But, sweetly as its answers will
Flatter hands of perfect skill,
It keeps its highest, holiest tone
For our belovèd Jane alone.

A Dirge

Rough wind, that moanest loud
    Grief too sad for song;
Wild wind, when sullen cloud
    Knells all the night long;
Sad storm, whose tears are vain,
Bare woods, whose branches strain,
Deep caves and dreary main, —
    Wail, for the world's wrong!

JOHN KEATS *(1795 – 1821)*

"To one who has been long in city pent"

To one who has been long in city pent,
   'Tis very sweet to look into the fair
   And open face of heaven, — to breathe a prayer
Full in the smile of the blue firmament.
Who is more happy, when, with heart's content,
   Fatigued he sinks into some pleasant lair
   Of wavy grass, and reads a debonair
And gentle tale of love and languishment?
Returning home at evening, with an ear
   Catching the notes of Philomel, — an eye
Watching the sailing cloudlet's bright career,
   He mourns that day so soon has glided by:
E'en like the passage of an angel's tear
   That falls through the clear ether silently.

On first looking into Chapman's Homer

Much have I travell'd in the realms of gold,
   And many goodly states and kingdoms seen;
   Round many western islands have I been
Which bards in fealty to Apollo hold.
Oft of one wide expanse had I been told
   That deep-brow'd Homer ruled as his demesne;
   Yet did I never breathe its pure serene
Till I heard Chapman speak out loud and bold:
Then felt I like some watcher of the skies
   When a new planet swims into his ken;
Or like stout Cortez when with eagle eyes
   He star'd at the Pacific — and all his men
Look'd at each other with a wild surmise —
   Silent, upon a peak in Darien.

"Happy is England! . . ."

Happy is England! I could be content
  To see no other verdure than its own;
  To feel no other breezes than are blown
Through its tall woods with high romances blent:
Yet do I sometimes feel a languishment
  For skies Italian, and an inward groan
  To sit upon an Alp as on a throne,
And half forget what world or worldling meant.
Happy is England, sweet her artless daughters;
  Enough their simple loveliness for me,
    Enough their whitest arms in silence clinging:
  Yet do I often warmly burn to see
    Beauties of deeper glance, and hear their singing,
And float with them about the summer waters.

Isabella; or, The Pot of Basil

A STORY FROM BOCCACCIO

I   Fair Isabel, poor simple Isabel!
      Lorenzo, a young palmer in Love's eye!
    They could not in the self-same mansion dwell
      Without some stir of heart, some malady;
    They could not sit at meals but feel how well
      It soothed each to be the other by;
    They could not, sure, beneath the same roof sleep
    But to each other dream, and nightly weep.

II   With every morn their love grew tenderer,
      With every eve deeper and tenderer still;
    He might not in house, field, or garden stir,
      But her full shape would all his seeing fill;
    And his continual voice was pleasanter
      To her, than noise of trees or hidden rill;
    Her lute-string gave an echo of his name,
    She spoilt her half-done broidery with the same.

III   He knew whose gentle hand was at the latch
      Before the door had given her to his eyes;
   And from her chamber-window he would catch
      Her beauty farther than the falcon spies;
   And constant as her vespers would he watch,
      Because her face was turn'd to the same skies;
   And with sick longing all the night outwear,
   To hear her morning-step upon the stair.

IV   A whole long month of May in this sad plight
      Made their cheeks paler by the break of June:
   'To-morrow will I bow to my delight,
      'To-morrow will I ask my lady's boon.' —
   'O may I never see another night,
      'Lorenzo, if thy lips breathe not love's tune.' —
   So spake they to their pillows; but, alas,
   Honeyless days and days did he let pass;

V   Until sweet Isabella's untouch'd cheek
      Fell sick within the rose's just domain,
   Fell thin as a young mother's, who doth seek
      By every lull to cool her infant's pain:
   'How ill she is,' said he, 'I may not speak,
      'And yet I will, and tell my love all plain:
   'If looks speak love-laws, I will drink her tears,
   'And at the least 'twill startle off her cares.'

VI   So said he one fair morning, and all day
      His heart beat awfully against his side;
   And to his heart he inwardly did pray
      For power to speak; but still the ruddy tide
   Stifled his voice, and puls'd resolve away —
      Fever'd his high conceit of such a bride,
   Yet brought him to the meekness of a child:
   Alas! when passion is both meek and wild!

VII   So once more he had wak'd and anguished
      A dreary night of love and misery,
   If Isabel's quick eye had not been wed
      To every symbol on his forehead high;
   She saw it waxing very pale and dead,
      And straight all flush'd; so, lisped tenderly,

'Lorenzo!' — here she ceas'd her timid quest,
But in her tone and look he read the rest.

VIII 'O Isabella, I can half perceive
     'That I may speak my grief into thine ear;
'If thou didst ever anything believe,
     'Believe how I love thee, believe how near
'My soul is to its doom: I would not grieve
     "Thy hand by unwelcome pressing, would not fear
'Thine eyes by gazing; but I cannot live
'Another night, and not my passion shrive.

IX 'Love! thou art leading me from wintry cold,
     'Lady! thou leadest me to summer clime,
'And I must taste the blossoms that unfold
     'In its ripe warmth this gracious morning time.'
So said, his erewhile timid lips grew bold,
     And poesied with hers in dewy rhyme:
Great bliss was with them, and great happiness
Grew, like a lusty flower in June's caress.

X Parting they seem'd to tread upon the air,
     Twin roses by the zephyr blown apart
Only to meet again more close, and share
     The inward fragrance of each other's heart.
She, to her chamber gone, a ditty fair
     Sang, of delicious love and honey'd dart;
He with light steps went up a western hill,
And bade the sun farewell, and joy'd his fill.

XI All close they met again, before the dusk
     Had taken from the stars its pleasant veil,
All close they met, all eves, before the dusk
     Had taken from the stars its pleasant veil,
Close in a bower of hyacinth and musk,
     Unknown of any, free from whispering tale.
Ah! better had it been for ever so,
Than idle ears should pleasure in their woe.

XII   Were they unhappy then? — It cannot be —
        Too many tears for lovers have been shed,
    Too many sighs give we to them in fee,
        Too much of pity after they are dead,
    Too many doleful stories do we see,
        Whose matter in bright gold were best be read;
    Except in such a page where Theseus' spouse
    Over the pathless waves towards him bows.

XIII   But, for the general award of love,
        The little sweet doth kill much bitterness;
    Though Dido silent is in under-grove,
        And Isabella's was a great distress,
    Though young Lorenzo in warm Indian clove
        Was not embalm'd, this truth is not the less —
    Even bees, the little almsmen of spring-bowers,
    Know there is richest juice in poison-flowers.

XIV   With her two brothers this fair lady dwelt,
        Enriched from ancestral merchandize,
    And for them many a weary hand did swelt
        In torched mines and noisy factories,
    And many once proud-quiver'd loins did melt
        In blood from stinging whip; — with hollow eyes
    Many all day in dazzling river stood,
    To take the rich-ored driftings of the flood.

XV   For them the Ceylon diver held his breath,
        And went all naked to the hungry shark;
    For them his ears gush'd blood; for them in death
        The seal on the cold ice with piteous bark
    Lay full of darts; for them alone did seethe
        A thousand men in troubles wide and dark:
    Half-ignorant, they turn'd an easy wheel,
    That set sharp racks at work, to pinch and peel.

XVI   Why were they proud? Because their marble founts
        Gush'd with more pride than do a wretch's tears? —

Why were they proud? Because fair orange-mounts
   Were of more soft ascent than lazar stairs? —
Why were they proud? Because red-lin'd accounts
   Were richer than the songs of Grecian years? —
Why were they proud? again we ask aloud,
Why in the name of Glory were they proud?

XVII Yet were these Florentines as self-retired
     In hungry pride and gainful cowardice,
As two close Hebrews in that land inspired,
     Paled in and vineyarded from beggar-spies;
The hawks of ship-mast forests — the untired
     And pannier'd mules for ducats and old lies —
Quick cat's-paws on the generous stray-away, —
Great wits in Spanish, Tuscan, and Malay.

XVIII How was it these same ledger-men could spy
     Fair Isabella in her downy nest?
How could they find out in Lorenzo's eye
     A straying from his toil? Hot Egypt's pest
Into their vision covetous and sly!
     How could these money-bags see east and west? —
Yet so they did — and every dealer fair
Must see behind, as doth the hunted hare.

XIX O eloquent and famed Boccaccio!
     Of thee we now should ask forgiving boon,
And of thy spicy myrtles as they blow,
     And of thy roses amorous of the moon,
And of thy lillies, that do paler grow
     Now they can no more hear thy ghittern's tune,
For venturing syllables that ill beseem
The quiet glooms of such a piteous theme.

XX Grant thou a pardon here, and then the tale
     Shall move on soberly, as it is meet;
There is no other crime, no mad assail
     To make old prose in modern rhyme more sweet:

But it is done — succeed the verse or fail —
    To honour thee, and thy gone spirit greet;
To stead thee as a verse in English tongue,
An echo of thee in the north-wind sung.

XXI   These brethren having found by many signs
        What love Lorenzo for their sister had,
And how she lov'd him too, each unconfines
        His bitter thoughts to other, well nigh mad
That he, the servant of their trade designs,
        Should in their sister's love be blithe and glad,
When 'twas their plan to coax her by degrees
To some high noble and his olive-trees.

XXII   And many a jealous conference had they,
        And many times they bit their lips alone,
Before they fix'd upon a surest way
        To make the youngster for his crime atone;
And at the last, these men of cruel clay
        Cut Mercy with a sharp knife to the bone;
For they resolved in some forest dim
To kill Lorenzo, and there bury him.

XXIII   So on a pleasant morning, as he leant
        Into the sun-rise, o'er the balustrade
Of the garden-terrace, towards him they bent
        Their footing through the dews; and to him said,
'You seem there in the quiet of content,
        'Lorenzo, and we are most loth to invade
'Calm speculation; but if you are wise,
        'Bestride your steed while cold is in the skies.

XXIV   'To-day we purpose, aye, this hour we mount
        'To spur three leagues towards the Apennine;
'Come down, we pray thee, ere the hot sun count
        'His dewy rosary on the eglantine.'
Lorenzo, courteously as he was wont,
        Bow'd a fair greeting to these serpents' whine;

And went in haste, to get in readiness,
· With belt, and spur, and bracing huntsman's dress.

XXV   And as he to the court-yard pass'd along,
    Each third step did he pause, and listen'd oft
If he could hear his lady's matin-song,
    Or the light whisper of her footstep soft;
And as he thus over his passion hung,
    He heard a laugh full musical aloft;
When, looking up, he saw her features bright
Smile through an in-door lattice, all delight.

XXVI   'Love, Isabel!' said he, 'I was in pain
    'Lest I should miss to bid thee a good morrow:
'Ah! what if I should lose thee, when so fain
    'I am to stifle all the heavy sorrow
'Of a poor three hours' absence? but we'll gain
    'Out of the amorous dark what day doth borrow.
'Good bye! I'll soon be back.' — 'Good bye!' said she: —
And as he went she chanted merrily.

XXVII   So the two brothers and their murder'd man
    Rode past fair Florence, to where Arno's stream
Gurgles through straiten'd banks, and still doth fan
    Itself with dancing bulrush, and the bream
Keeps head against the freshets. Sick and wan
    The brothers' faces in the ford did seem,
Lorenzo's flush with love. — They pass'd the water
Into a forest quiet for the slaughter.

XXVIII There was Lorenzo slain and buried in,
    There in that forest did his great love cease;
Ah! when a soul doth thus its freedom win,
    It aches in loneliness — is ill at peace
As the break-covert blood-hounds of such sin:
    They dipp'd their swords in the water, and did tease
Their horses homeward, with convulsed spur,
Each richer by his being a murderer.

XXIX   They told their sister how, with sudden speed,
        Lorenzo had ta'en ship for foreign lands,
    Because of some great urgency and need
        In their affairs, requiring trusty hands.
    Poor Girl! put on thy stifling widow's weed,
        And 'scape at once from Hope's accursed bands;
    To-day thou wilt not see him, nor to-morrow,
    And the next day will be a day of sorrow.

XXX   She weeps alone for pleasures not to be;
        Sorely she wept until the night came on,
    And then, instead of love, O misery!
        She brooded o'er the luxury alone:
    His image in the dusk she seem'd to see,
        And to the silence made a gentle moan,
    Spreading her perfect arms upon the air,
    And on her couch low murmuring, 'Where? O where?'

XXXI   But Selfishness, Love's cousin, held not long
        Its fiery vigil in her single breast;
    She fretted for the golden hour, and hung
        Upon the time with feverish unrest —
    Not long — for soon into her heart a throng
        Of higher occupants, a richer zest,
    Came tragic; passion not to be subdued,
    And sorrow for her love in travels rude.

XXXII   In the mid days of autumn, on their eves
        The breath of Winter comes from far away,
    And the sick west continually bereaves
        Of some gold tinge, and plays a roundelay
    Of death among the bushes and the leaves,
        To make all bare before he dares to stray
    From his north cavern. So sweet Isabel
    By gradual decay from beauty fell,

XXXIII   Because Lorenzo came not. Oftentimes
        She ask'd her brothers, with an eye all pale,

Striving to be itself, what dungeon climes
  Could keep him off so long? They spake a tale
Time after time, to quiet her. Their crimes
  Came on them, like a smoke from Hinnom's vale;
And every night in dreams they groan'd aloud,
To see their sister in her snowy shroud.

XXXIV   And she had died in drowsy ignorance,
  But for a thing more deadly dark than all;
It came like a fierce potion, drunk by chance,
  Which saves a sick man from the feather'd pall
For some few gasping moments; like a lance,
  Waking an Indian from his cloudy hall
With cruel pierce, and bringing him again
Sense of the gnawing fire at heart and brain.

XXXV   It was a vision. — In the drowsy gloom,
  The dull of midnight, at her couch's foot
Lorenzo stood, and wept: the forest tomb
  Had marr'd his glossy hair which once could shoot
Lustre into the sun, and put cold doom
  Upon his lips, and taken the soft lute
From his lorn voice, and past his loamed ears
Had made a miry channel for his tears.

XXXVI   Strange sound it was, when the pale shadow spake;
  For there was striving, in its piteous tongue,
To speak as when on earth it was awake,
  And Isabella on its music hung:
Languor there was in it, and tremulous shake,
  As in a palsied Druid's harp unstrung;
And through it moan'd a ghostly under-song,
Like hoarse night-gusts sepulchral briars among.

XXXVII   Its eyes, though wild, were still all dewy bright
  With love, and kept all phantom fear aloof
From the poor girl by magic of their light,
  The while it did unthread the horrid woof
Of the late darken'd time, — the murderous spite
  Of pride and avarice, — the dark pine roof

In the forest, — and the sodden turfed dell,
Where, without any word, from stabs he fell.

XXXVIII   Saying moreover, 'Isabel, my sweet!
     'Red whortle-berries droop above my head,
   'And a large flint-stone weighs upon my feet;
     'Around me beeches and high chestnuts shed
   'Their leaves and prickly nuts; a sheep-fold bleat
     'Comes from beyond the river to my bed:
   'Go, shed one tear upon my heather-bloom,
   'And it shall comfort me within the tomb.

XXXIX   'I am a shadow now, alas! alas!
     'Upon the skirts of human-nature dwelling
   'Alone: I chant alone the holy mass,
     'While little sounds of life are round me knelling,
   'And glossy bees at noon do fieldward pass,
     'And many a chapel bell the hour is telling,
   'Paining me through: those sounds grow strange to me,
   'And thou are distant in Humanity.

XL   'I know what was, I feel full well what is,
     'And I should rage, if spirits could go mad;
   'Though I forget the taste of earthly bliss,
     'That paleness warms my grave, as though I had
   'A Seraph chosen from the bright abyss
     'To be my spouse: thy paleness makes me glad;
   'Thy beauty grows upon me, and I feel
   'A greater love through all my essence steal.'

XLI   The Spirit mourn'd 'Adieu!' — dissolv'd and left
     The atom darkness in a slow turmoil;
   As when of healthful midnight sleep bereft,
     Thinking on rugged hours and fruitless toil,
   We put our eyes into a pillowy cleft,
     And see the spangly gloom froth up and boil:
   It made sad Isabella's eyelids ache,
   And in the dawn she started up awake;

XLII   'Ha! ha!' said she, 'I knew not this hard life,
   'I thought the worst was simple misery;
  'I thought some Fate with pleasure or with strife
   'Portion'd us — happy days, or else to die;
  'But there is crime — a brother's bloody knife!
   'Sweet Spirit, thou hast school'd my infancy:
  'I'll visit thee for this, and kiss thine eyes,
  'And greet thee morn and even in the skies.'

XLIII   When the full morning came, she had devised
   How she might secret to the forest hie;
  How she might find the clay, so dearly prized,
   And sing to it one latest lullaby;
  How her short absence might be unsurmised,
   While she the inmost of the dream would try.
  Resolv'd, she took with her an aged nurse,
  And went into that dismal forest-hearse.

XLIV   See, as they creep along the river side,
   How she doth whisper to that aged Dame,
  And, after looking round the champaign wide,
   Shows her a knife. — 'What feverous hectic flame
  'Burns in thee, child? — What good can thee betide,
   'That thou should'st smile again?' — The evening came,
  And they had found Lorenzo's earthy bed;
  The flint was there, the berries at his head.

XLV   Who hath not loiter'd in a green church-yard,
   And let his spirit, like a demon-mole,
  Work through the clayey soil and gravel hard,
   To see scull, coffin'd bones, and funeral stole;
  Pitying each form that hungry Death hath marr'd
   And filling it once more with human soul?
  Ah! this is holiday to what was felt
  When Isabella by Lorenzo knelt.

XLVI   She gaz'd into the fresh-thrown mould, as though
   One glance did fully all its secrets tell;
  Clearly she saw, as other eyes would know
   Pale limbs at bottom of a crystal well;

Upon the murderous spot she seem'd to grow,
    Like to a native lilly of the dell:
Then with her knife, all sudden, she began
To dig more fervently than misers can.

XLVII   Soon she turn'd up a soiled glove, whereon
    Her silk had play'd in purple phantasies,
She kiss'd it with a lip more chill than stone,
    And put it in her bosom, where it dries
And freezes utterly unto the bone
    Those dainties made to still an infant's cries:
Then 'gan she work again; nor stay'd her care,
But to throw back at times her veiling hair.

XLVIII   That old nurse stood beside her wondering,
    Until her heart felt pity to the core
At sight of such a dismal labouring,
    And so she kneeled, with her locks all hoar,
And put her lean hands to the horrid thing:
    Three hours they labour'd at this travail sore;
At last they felt the kernel of the grave,
And Isabella did not stamp and rave.

XLIX   Ah! wherefore all this wormy circumstance?
    Why linger at the yawning tomb so long?
O for the gentleness of old Romance,
    The simple plaining of a minstrel's song!
Fair reader, at the old tale take a glance,
    For here, in truth, it doth not well belong
To speak: — O turn thee to the very tale,
And taste the music of that vision pale.

L   With duller steel than the Perséan sword
    They cut away no formless monster's head,
But one, whose gentleness did well accord
    With death, as life. The ancient harps have said,
Love never dies, but lives, immortal Lord:
    If Love impersonate was ever dead,
Pale Isabella kiss'd it, and low moan'd.
'Twas love; cold, — dead indeed, but not dethroned.

LI   In anxious secrecy they took it home,
     And then the prize was all for Isabel:
She calm'd its wild hair with a golden comb,
     And all around each eye's sepulchral cell
Pointed each fringed lash; the smeared loam
     With tears, as chilly as a dripping well,
She drench'd away: — and still she comb'd, and kept
Sighing all day — and still she kiss'd, and wept.

LII   Then in a silken scarf, — sweet with the dews
     Of precious flowers pluck'd in Araby,
And divine liquids come with odorous ooze
     Through the cold serpent-pipe refreshfully, —
She wrapp'd it up; and for its tomb did choose
     A garden-pot, wherein she laid it by,
And cover'd it with mould, and o'er it set
Sweet Basil, which her tears kept ever wet.

LIII And she forgot the stars, the moon, and sun,
     And she forgot the blue above the trees,
And she forgot the dells where waters run,
     And she forgot the chilly autumn breeze;
She had no knowledge when the day was done,
     And the new morn she saw not: but in peace
Hung over her sweet Basil evermore,
And moisten'd it with tears unto the core.

LIV   And so she ever fed it with thin tears,
     Whence thick, and green, and beautiful it grew,
So that it smelt more balmy than its peers
     Of Basil-tufts in Florence; for it drew
Nurture besides, and life, from human fears,
     From the fast mouldering head there shut from view:
So that the jewel, safely casketed,
Came forth, and in perfumed leafits spread.

LV   O Melancholy, linger here awhile!
     O Music, Music, breathe despondingly!

O Echo, Echo, from some sombre isle,
    Unknown, Lethean, sigh to us — O sigh!
Spirits in grief, lift up your heads, and smile;
    Lift up your heads, sweet Spirits, heavily,
And make a pale light in your cypress glooms,
Tinting with silver wan your marble tombs.

LVI   Moan hither, all ye syllables of woe,
    From the deep throat of sad Melpomene!
Through bronzed lyre in tragic order go,
    And touch the strings into a mystery;
Sound mournfully upon the winds and low;
    For simple Isabel is soon to be ·
Among the dead: She withers, like a palm
Cut by an Indian for its juicy balm.

LVII   O leave the palm to wither by itself;
    Let not quick Winter chill its dying hour! —
It may not be — those Baälites of pelf,
    Her brethren, noted the continual shower
From her dead eyes; and many a curious elf,
    Among her kindred, wonder'd that such dower
Of youth and beauty should be thrown aside
By one mark'd out to be a Noble's bride.

LVIII And, furthermore, her brethren wonder'd much
    Why she sat drooping by the Basil green,
And why it flourish'd, as by magic touch;
    Greatly they wonder'd what the thing might mean:
They could not surely give belief, that such
    A very nothing would have power to wean
Her from her own fair youth, and pleasures gay,
And even remembrance of her love's delay.

LIX   Therefore they watch'd a time when they might sift
    This hidden whim; and long they watch'd in vain;
For seldom did she go to chapel-shrift,
    And seldom felt she any hunger-pain;
And when she left, she hurried back, as swift

As bird on wing to breast its eggs again;
And, patient as a hen-bird, sat her there
Beside her Basil, weeping through her hair.

LX   Yet they contriv'd to steal the Basil-pot,
          And to examine it in secret place;
      The thing was vile with green and livid spot,
          And yet they knew it was Lorenzo's face:
      The guerdon of their murder they had got,
          And so left Florence in a moment's space,
      Never to turn again. — Away they went,
      With blood upon their heads, to banishment.

LXI   O Melancholy, turn thine eyes away!
          O Music, Music, breathe despondingly!
      O Echo, Echo, on some other day,
          From isles Lethean, sigh to us — O sigh!
      Spirits of grief, sing not your 'Well-a-way!'
          For Isabel, sweet Isabel, will die;
      Will die a death too lone and incomplete,
      Now they have ta'en away her Basil sweet.

LXII Piteous she look'd on dead and senseless things,
          Asking for her lost Basil amorously;
      And with melodious chuckle in the strings
          Of her lorn voice, she oftentimes would cry
      After the Pilgrim in his wanderings,
          To ask him where her Basil was; and why
      'Twas hid from her: 'For cruel 'tis,' said she,
      'To steal my Basil-pot away from me.'

LXIII And so she pined, and so she died forlorn,
          Imploring for her Basil to the last.
      No heart was there in Florence but did mourn
          In pity of her love, so overcast.
      And a sad ditty of this story born
          From mouth to mouth through all the country pass'd:
      Still is the burthen sung — 'O cruelty,
      'To steal my Basil-pot away from me!'

The Eve of St. Agnes

I St. Agnes' Eve — Ah, bitter chill it was!
   The owl, for all his feathers, was a-cold;
   The hare limp'd trembling through the frozen grass,
   And silent was the flock in woolly fold:
   Numb were the Beadsman's fingers, while he told
   His rosary, and while his frosted breath,
   Like pious incense from a censer old,
   Seem'd taking flight for heaven, without a death,
  Past the sweet Virgin's picture, while his prayer he saith.

II His prayer he saith, this patient, holy man;
   Then takes his lamp, and riseth from his knees,
   And back returneth, meagre, barefoot, wan,
   Along the chapel aisle by slow degrees:
   The sculptur'd dead, on each side, seem to freeze,
   Emprison'd in black, purgatorial rails:
   Knights, ladies, praying in dumb orat'ries,
   He passeth by; and his weak spirit fails
  To think how they may ache in icy hoods and mails.

III Northward he turneth through a little door,
   And scarce three steps, ere Music's golden tongue
   Flatter'd to tears this aged man and poor;
   But no — already had his deathbell rung:
   The joys of all his life were said and sung:
   His was harsh penance on St. Agnes' Eve:
   Another way he went, and soon among
   Rough ashes sat he for his soul's reprieve,
  And all night kept awake, for sinners' sake to grieve.

IV That ancient Beadsman heard the prelude soft;
   And so it chanc'd, for many a door was wide,
   From hurry to and fro. Soon, up aloft,
   The silver, snarling trumpets 'gan to chide:
   The level chambers, ready with their pride,

Were glowing to receive a thousand guests:
The carved angels, ever eager-eyed,
Star'd, where upon their heads the cornice rests,
With hair blown back, and wings put cross-wise on their breasts.

V   At length burst in the argent revelry,
With plume, tiara, and all rich array,
Numerous as shadows haunting faerily
The brain, new stuff'd, in youth, with triumphs gay
Of old romance. These let us wish away,
And turn, sole-thoughted, to one Lady there,
Whose heart had brooded, all that wintry day,
On love, and wing'd St. Agnes' saintly care,
As she had heard old dames full many times declare.

VI   They told her how, upon St. Agnes' Eve,
Young virgins might have visions of delight,
And soft adorings from their loves receive
Upon the honey'd middle of the night,
If ceremonies due they did aright;
As, supperless to bed they must retire,
And couch supine their beauties, lilly white;
Nor look behind, nor sideways, but require
Of Heaven with upward eyes for all that they desire.

VII   Full of this whim was thoughtful Madeline:
The music, yearning like a God in pain,
She scarcely heard: her maiden eyes divine,
Fix'd on the floor, saw many a sweeping train
Pass by — she heeded not at all: in vain
Came many a tiptoe, amorous cavalier,
And back retir'd; not cool'd by high disdain,
But she saw not: her heart was otherwhere:
She sigh'd for Agnes' dreams, the sweetest of the year.

VIII   She danc'd along with vague, regardless eyes,
Anxious her lips, her breathing quick and short:

The hallow'd hour was near at hand: she sighs
Amid the timbrels, and the throng'd resort
Of whisperers in anger, or in sport;
'Mid looks of love, defiance, hate, and scorn,
Hoodwink'd with faery fancy; all amort,
Save to St. Agnes and her lambs unshorn,
And all the bliss to be before to-morrow morn.

IX   So, purposing each moment to retire,
She linger'd still. Meantime, across the moors,
Had come young Porphyro, with heart on fire
For Madeline. Beside the portal doors,
Buttress'd from moonlight, stands he, and implores
All saints to give him sight of Madeline,
But for one moment in the tedious hours,
That he might gaze and worship all unseen;
Perchance speak, kneel, touch, kiss — in sooth such things have been.

X   He ventures in: let no buzz'd whisper tell:
All eyes be muffled, or a hundred swords
Will storm his heart, Love's fev'rous citadel:
For him, those chambers held barbarian hordes,
Hyena foemen, and hot-blooded lords,
Whose very dogs would execrations howl
Against his lineage: not one breast affords
Him any mercy, in that mansion foul,
Save one old beldame, weak in body and in soul.

XI   Ah, happy chance! the aged creature came,
Shuffling along with ivory-headed wand,
To where he stood, hid from the torch's flame,
Behind a broad hall-pillar, far beyond
The sound of merriment and chorus bland:
He startled her; but soon she knew his face,
And grasp'd his fingers in her palsied hand,
Saying, 'Mercy, Porphyro! hie thee from this place:
'They are all here to-night, the whole blood-thirsty race!

XII   'Get hence! get hence! there's dwarfish Hildebrand;
            'He had a fever late, and in the fit
            'He cursed thee and thine, both house and land:
            'Then there's that old Lord Maurice, not a whit
            'More tame for his gray hairs — Alas me! flit!
            'Flit like a ghost away.' — 'Ah, Gossip dear,
            'We're safe enough; here in this arm-chair sit,
            'And tell me how' — 'Good Saints! not here, not here;
      'Follow me, child, or else these stones will be thy bier.'

XIII   He follow'd through a lowly arched way,
            Brushing the cobwebs with his lofty plume,
            And as she mutter'd 'Well-a — well-a-day!'
            He found him in a little moonlight room,
            Pale, lattic'd, chill, and silent as a tomb.
            'Now tell me where is Madeline,' said he,
            'O tell me, Angela, by the holy loom
            'Which none but secret sisterhood may see,
      'When they St. Agnes' wool are weaving piously.'

XIV   'St. Agnes! Ah! it is St. Agnes' Eve —
            'Yet men will murder upon holy days:
            'Thou must hold water in a witch's sieve,
            'And be liege-lord of all the Elves and Fays,
            'To venture so: it fills me with amaze
            'To see thee, Porphyro! — St. Agnes' Eve!
            'God's help! my lady fair the conjuror plays
            'This very night: good angels her deceive!
      'But let me laugh awhile, I've mickle time to grieve.'

XV   Feebly she laugheth in the languid moon,
            While Porphyro upon her face doth look,
            Like puzzled urchin on an aged crone
            Who keepeth clos'd a wond'rous riddle-book,
            As spectacled she sits in chimney nook.
            But soon his eyes grew brilliant, when she told
            His lady's purpose; and he scarce could brook

Tears, at the thought of those enchantments cold,
And Madeline asleep in lap of legends old.

XVI Sudden a thought came like a full-blown rose,
  Flushing his brow, and in his pained heart
  Made purple riot: then doth he propose
  A strategem, that makes the beldame start:
  'A cruel man and impious thou art:
  'Sweet lady, let her pray, and sleep, and dream
  'Alone with her good angels, far apart
  'From wicked men like thee. Go, go! — I deem
'Thou canst not surely be the same that thou didst seem.'

XVII 'I will not harm her, by all saints I swear,'
  Quoth Porphyro: 'O may I ne'er find grace
  'When my weak voice shall whisper its last prayer,
  'If one of her soft ringlets I displace,
  'Or look with ruffian passion in her face:
  'Good Angela, believe me by these tears;
  'Or I will, even in a moment's space,
  'Awake, with horrid shout, my foemen's ears,
'And beard them, though they be more fang'd than wolves and
   bears.'

XVIII 'Ah! why wilt thou affright a feeble soul?
  'A poor, weak, palsy-stricken, churchyard thing,
  'Whose passing-bell may ere the midnight toll;
  'Whose prayers for thee, each morn and evening,
  'Were never miss'd.' — Thus plaining, doth she bring
  A gentler speech from burning Porphyro;
  So woful, and of such deep sorrowing,
  That Angela gives promise she will do
Whatever he shall wish, betide her weal or woe.

XIX Which was, to lead him, in close secrecy,
  Even to Madeline's chamber, and there hide
  Him in a closet, of such privacy
  That he might see her beauty unespied,
  And win perhaps that night a peerless bride,

While legion'd faeries pac'd the coverlet,
And pale enchantment held her sleepy-eyed.
Never on such a night have lovers met,
Since Merlin paid his Demon all the monstrous debt.

XX   'It shall be as thou wishest,' said the Dame:
'All cates and dainties shall be stored there
'Quickly on this feast-night: by the tambour frame
'Her own lute thou wilt see: no time to spare,
'For I am slow and feeble, and scarce dare
'On such a catering trust my dizzy head.
'Wait here, my child, with patience; kneel· in prayer
'The while: Ah! thou must needs the lady wed,
'Or may I never leave my grave among the dead.'

XXI   So saying, she hobbled off with busy fear.
The lover's endless minutes slowly pass'd;
The dame return'd, and whisper'd in his ear
To follow her; with aged eyes aghast
From fright of dim espial. Safe at last,
Through many a dusky gallery, they gain
The maiden's chamber, silken, hush'd, and chaste;
Where Porphyro took covert, pleas'd amain.
His poor guide hurried back with agues in her brain.

XXII   Her falt'ring hand upon the balustrade,
Old Angela was feeling for the stair,
When Madeline, St. Agnes' charmed maid,
Rose, like a mission'd spirit, unaware:
With silver taper's light, and pious care,
She turn'd, and down the aged gossip led
To a safe level matting. Now prepare,
Young Porphyro, for gazing on that bed;
She comes, she comes again, like ring-dove fray'd and fled.

XXIII   Out went the taper as she hurried in;
Its little smoke, in pallid moonshine, died:
She clos'd the door, she panted, all akin
To spirits of the air, and visions wide:

No uttered syllable, or, woe betide!
But to her heart, her heart was voluble,
Paining with eloquence her balmy side;
As though a tongueless nightingale should swell
Her throat in vain, and die, heart-stifled, in her dell.

XXIV   A casement high and triple-arch'd there was,
            All garlanded with carven imag'ries
            Of fruits, and flowers, and bunches of knot-grass,
            And diamonded with panes of quaint device,
            Innumerable of stains and splendid dyes,
            As are the tiger-moth's deep-damask'd wings;
            And in the midst, 'mong thousand heraldries,
            And twilight saints, and dim emblazonings,
        A shielded scutcheon blush'd with blood of queens and kings.

XXV   Full on this casement shone the wintry moon,
            And threw warm gules on Madeline's fair breast,
            As down she knelt for heaven's grace and boon;
            Rose-bloom fell on her hands, together prest,
            And on her silver cross soft amethyst,
            And on her hair a glory, like a saint:
            She seem'd a splendid angel, newly drest,
            Save wings, for heaven: — Porphyro grew faint:
        She knelt, so pure a thing, so free from mortal taint.

XXVI   Anon his heart revives: her vespers done,
            Of all its wreathed pearls her hair she frees;
            Unclasps her warmed jewels one by one;
            Loosens her fragrant boddice; by degrees
            Her rich attire creeps rustling to her knees:
            Half-hidden, like a mermaid in sea-weed,
            Pensive awhile she dreams awake, and sees,
            In fancy, fair St. Agnes in her bed,
        But dares not look behind, or all the charm is fled.

XXVII   Soon, trembling in her soft and chilly nest,
            In sort of wakeful swoon, perplex'd she lay,

Until the poppied warmth of sleep oppress'd
Her soothed limbs, and soul fatigued away;
Flown, like a thought, until the morrow-day;
Blissfully haven'd both from joy and pain;
Clasp'd like a missal where swart Paynims pray;
Blinded alike from sunshine and from rain,
As though a rose should shut, and be a bud again.

XXVIII   Stol'n to this paradise, and so entranced,
Porphyro gazed upon her empty dress,
And listen'd to her breathing, if it chanced
To wake into a slumberous tenderness;
Which when he heard, that minute did he bless,
And breath'd himself: then from the closet crept,
Noiseless as fear in a wide wilderness,
And over the hush'd carpet, silent, stept,
And 'tween the curtains peep'd, where, lo! — how fast she slept.

XXIX   Then by the bed-side, where the faded moon
Made a dim, silver twilight, soft he set
A table, and, half anguish'd, threw thereon
A cloth of woven crimson, gold, and jet: —
O for some drowsy Morphean amulet!
The boisterous, midnight, festive clarion,
The kettle-drum, and far-heard clarinet,
Affray his ears, though but in dying tone: —
The hall door shuts again, and all the noise is gone.

XXX   And still she slept an azure-lidded sleep,
In blanched linen, smooth, and lavender'd,
While he from forth the closet brought a heap
Of candied apple, quince, and plum, and gourd;
With jellies soother than the creamy curd,
And lucent syrops, tinct with cinnamon;
Manna and dates, in argosy transferr'd
From Fez; and spiced dainties, every one,
From silken Samarcand to cedar'd Lebanon.

XXXI   These delicates he heap'd with glowing hand
          On golden dishes and in baskets bright
          Of wreathed silver: sumptuous they stand
          In the retired quiet of the night,
          Filling the chilly room with perfume light. —
          'And now, my love, my seraph fair, awake!
          'Thou art my heaven, and I thine eremite:
          'Open thine eyes, for meek St. Agnes' sake,
      'Or I shall drowse beside thee, so my soul doth ache.'

XXXII   Thus whispering, his warm, unnerved arm
          Sank in her pillow. Shaded was her dream
          By the dusk curtains: — 'twas a midnight charm
          Impossible to melt as iced stream:
          The lustrous salvers in the moonlight gleam;
          Broad golden fringe upon the carpet lies:
          It seem'd he never, never could redeem
          From such a stedfast spell his lady's eyes;
      So mus'd awhile, entoil'd in woofed phantasies.

XXXIII   Awakening up, he took her hollow lute, —
          Tumultuous, — and, in chords that tenderest be,
          He play'd an ancient ditty, long since mute,
          In Provence call'd, 'La belle dame sans mercy:'
          Close to her ear touching the melody; —
          Wherewith disturb'd, she utter'd a soft moan:
          He ceased — she panted quick — and suddenly
          Her blue affrayed eyes wide open shone:
      Upon his knees he sank, pale as smooth-sculptured stone.

XXXIV   Her eyes were open, but she still beheld,
          Now wide awake, the vision of her sleep:
          There was a painful change, that nigh expell'd
          The blisses of her dream so pure and deep
          At which fair Madeline began to weep,
          And moan forth witless words with many a sigh;
          While still her gaze on Porphyro would keep;

Who knelt, with joined hands and piteous eye,
Fearing to move or speak, she look'd so dreamingly.

XXXV   'Ah, Porphyro!' said she, 'but even now
'Thy voice was at sweet tremble in mine ear,
'Made tuneable with every sweetest vow;
'And those sad eyes were spiritual and clear:
'How chang'd thou art! how pallid, chill, and drear!
'Give me that voice again, my Porphyro,
'Those looks immortal, those complainings dear!
'Oh leave me not in this eternal woe,
'For if thou diest, my Love, I know not where to go.'

XXXVI   Beyond a mortal man impassion'd far
At these voluptuous accents, he arose,
Ethereal, flush'd, and like a throbbing star
Seen mid the sapphire heaven's deep repose;
Into her dream he melted, as the rose
Blendeth its odour with the violet, —
Solution sweet: meantime the frost-wind blows
Like Love's alarum pattering the sharp sleet
Against the window-panes; St. Agnes' moon hath set.

XXXVII   'Tis dark: quick pattereth the flaw-blown sleet:
'This is no dream, my bride, my Madeline!'
'Tis dark: the iced gusts still rave and beat:
'No dream, alas! alas! and woe is mine!
'Porphyro will leave me here to fade and pine. —
'Cruel! what traitor could thee hither bring?
'I curse not, for my heart is lost in thine,
'Though thou forsakest a deceived thing; —
'A dove forlorn and lost with sick unpruned wing.'

XXXVIII   'My Madeline! sweet dreamer! lovely bride!
'Say, may I be for aye thy vassal blest?
'Thy beauty's shield, heart-shap'd and vermeil dyed?
'Ah, silver shrine, here will I take my rest
'After so many hours of toil and quest,
'A famish'd pilgrim, — sav'd by miracle.

'Though I have found, I will not rob thy nest
'Saving of thy sweet self; if thou think'st well
'To trust, fair Madeline, to no rude infidel.

XXXIX   'Hark! 'tis an elfin-storm from faery land,
'Of haggard seeming, but a boon indeed:
'Arise — arise! the morning is at hand; —
'The bloated wassaillers will never heed: —
'Let us away, my love, with happy speed;
'There are no ears to hear, or eyes to see, —
'Drown'd all in Rhenish and the sleepy mead:
'Awake! arise! my love, and fearless be,
'For o'er the southern moors I have a home for thee.'

XL   She hurried at his words, beset with fears,
For there were sleeping dragons all around,
At glaring watch, perhaps, with ready spears —
Down the wide stairs a darkling way they found. —
In all the house was heard no human sound.
A chain-droop'd lamp was flickering by each door;
The arras, rich with horseman, hawk, and hound,
Flutter'd in the besieging wind's uproar;
And the long carpets rose along the gusty floor.

XLI   They glide, like phantoms, into the wide hall;
Like phantoms, to the iron porch, they glide;
Where lay the Porter, in uneasy sprawl,
With a huge empty flaggon by his side:
The wakeful bloodhound rose, and shook his hide,
But his sagacious eye an inmate owns:
By one, and one, the bolts full easy slide: —
The chains lie silent on the footworn stones; —
The key turns, and the door upon its hinges groans.

XLII   And they are gone: aye, ages long ago
These lovers fled away into the storm.
That night the Baron dreamt of many a woe,
And all his warrior-guests, with shade and form
Of witch, and demon, and large coffin-worm,

Were long be-nightmar'd. Angela the old
Died palsy-twitch'd, with meagre face deform;
The Beadsman, after thousand aves told,
For aye unsought for slept among his ashes cold.

Ode to a Nightingale

I   My heart aches, and a drowsy numbness pains
    My sense, as though of hemlock I had drunk,
Or emptied some dull opiate to the drains
    One minute past, and Lethe-wards had sunk:
'Tis not through envy of thy happy lot,
    But being too happy in thine happiness, —
        That thou, light-winged Dryad of the trees,
            In some melodious plot
    Of beechen green, and shadows numberless,
        Singest of summer in full-throated ease.

II   O, for a draught of vintage! that hath been
    Cool'd a long age in the deep-delved earth,
Tasting of Flora and the country green,
    Dance, and Provençal song, and sunburnt mirth!
O for a beaker full of the warm South,
    Full of the true, the blushful Hippocrene,
        With beaded bubbles winking at the brim,
            And purple-stained mouth;
    That I might drink, and leave the world unseen,
        And with thee fade away into the forest dim:

III   Fade far away, dissolve, and quite forget
    What thou among the leaves hast never known,
The weariness, the fever, and the fret
    Here, where men sit and hear each other groan;
Where palsy shakes a few, sad, last gray hairs,
    Where youth grows pale, and spectre-thin, and dies;
        Where but to think is to be full of sorrow
            And leaden-eyed despairs,

Where Beauty cannot keep her lustrous eyes,
   Or new Love pine at them beyond to-morrow.

IV   Away! away! for I will fly to thee,
       Not charioted by Bacchus and his pards,
   But on the viewless wings of Poesy,
       Though the dull brain perplexes and retards:
   Already with thee! tender is the night,
       And haply the Queen-Moon is on her throne,
           Cluster'd around by all her starry Fays;
                But here there is no light,
           Save what from heaven is with the breezes blown
               Through verdurous glooms and winding mossy ways.

V   I cannot see what flowers are at my feet,
       Nor what soft incense hangs upon the boughs,
   But, in embalmed darkness, guess each sweet
       Wherewith the seasonable month endows
   The grass, the thicket, and the fruit-tree wild;
       White hawthorn, and the pastoral eglantine;
           Fast fading violets cover'd up in leaves;
                And mid-May's eldest child,
           The coming musk-rose, full of dewy wine,
               The murmurous haunt of flies on summer eves.

VI   Darkling I listen; and, for many a time
       I have been half in love with easeful Death,
   Call'd him soft names in many a mused rhyme,
       To take into the air my quiet breath;
   Now more than ever seems it rich to die,
       To cease upon the midnight with no pain,
           While thou art pouring forth thy soul abroad
                In such an ecstasy!
           Still wouldst thou sing, and I have ears in vain —
               To thy high requiem become a sod.

VII   Thou wast not born for death, immortal Bird!
       No hungry generations tread thee down;
   The voice I hear this passing night was heard

In ancient days by emperor and clown:
Perhaps the self-same song that found a path
   Through the sad heart of Ruth, when, sick for home,
      She stood in tears amid the alien corn;
         The same that oft-times hath
      Charm'd magic casements, opening on the foam
         Of perilous seas, in faery lands forlorn.

VIII   Forlorn! the very word is like a bell
      To toll me back from thee to my sole self!
   Adieu! the fancy cannot cheat so well
      As she is fam'd to do, deceiving elf.
   Adieu! adieu! thy plaintive anthem fades
      Past the near meadows, over the still stream,
         Up the hill-side; and now 'tis buried deep
            In the next valley-glades:
         Was it a vision, or a waking dream?
            Fled is that music: — Do I wake or sleep?

Ode on a Grecian Urn

I   Thou still unravish'd bride of quietness,
      Thou foster-child of silence and slow time,
   Sylvan historian, who canst thus express
      A flowery tale more sweetly than our rhyme:
   What leaf-fring'd legend haunts about thy shape
      Of deities or mortals, or of both,
         In Tempe or the dales of Arcady?
      What men or gods are these? What maidens loth?
   What mad pursuit? What struggle to escape?
      What pipes and timbrels? What wild ecstasy?

II   Heard melodies are sweet, but those unheard
      Are sweeter; therefore, ye soft pipes, play on;
   Not to the sensual ear, but, more endear'd,
      Pipe to the spirit ditties of no tone:

Fair youth, beneath the trees, thou canst not leave
　　Thy song, nor ever can those trees be bare;
　　　　Bold Lover, never, never canst thou kiss,
　　Though winning near the goal — yet, do not grieve;
　　　　She cannot fade, though thou hast not thy bliss,
　　　　　　For ever wilt thou love, and she be fair!

III　Ah, happy, happy boughs! that cannot shed
　　Your leaves, nor ever bid the Spring adieu;
　　And, happy melodist, unwearied,
　　　For ever piping songs for ever new;
　　More happy love! more happy, happy love!
　　　For ever warm and still to be enjoy'd,
　　　　For ever panting, and for ever young;
　　All breathing human passion far above,
　　　That leaves a heart high-sorrowful and cloy'd,
　　　　A burning forehead, and a parching tongue.

IV　Who are these coming to the sacrifice?
　　To what green altar, O mysterious priest,
　　Lead'st thou that heifer lowing at the skies,
　　　And all her silken flanks with garlands drest?
　　What little town by river or sea shore,
　　　Or mountain-built with peaceful citadel,
　　　　Is emptied of this folk, this pious morn?
　　And, little town, thy streets for evermore
　　　Will silent be; and not a soul to tell
　　　　Why thou art desolate, can e'er return.

V　O Attic shape! Fair attitude! with brede
　　Of marble men and maidens overwrought,
　　With forest branches and the trodden weed;
　　　Thou, silent form, dost tease us out of thought
　　As doth eternity: Cold Pastoral!
　　　When old age shall this generation waste,
　　　　Thou shalt remain, in midst of other woe
　　Than ours, a friend to man, to whom thou say'st,
　　　'Beauty is truth, truth beauty,' — that is all
　　　　Ye know on earth, and all ye need to know.

Ode to Psyche

O Goddess! hear these tuneless numbers, wrung
   By sweet enforcement and remembrance dear,
And pardon that thy secrets should be sung
   Even into thine own soft-conched ear:
Surely I dreamt to-day, or did I see
   The winged Psyche with awaken'd eyes?
I wander'd in a forest thoughtlessly,
   And, on the sudden, fainting with surprise,
Saw two fair creatures, couched side by side
   In deepest grass, beneath the whisp'ring roof
   Of leaves and trembled blossoms, where there ran
      A brooklet, scarce espied:

'Mid hush'd, cool-rooted flowers, fragrant-eyed,
   Blue, silver-white, and budded Tyrian,
They lay calm-breathing on the bedded grass;
   Their arms embraced, and their pinions too;
   Their lips touch'd not, but had not bade adieu,
As if disjoined by soft-handed slumber,
And ready still past kisses to outnumber
   At tender eye-dawn of aurorean love:
      The winged boy I knew;
   But who wast thou, O happy, happy dove?
      His Psyche true!

O latest born and loveliest vision far
   Of all Olympus' faded hierarchy!
Fairer than Phœbe's sapphire-region'd star,
   Or Vesper, amorous glow-worm of the sky;
Fairer than these, though temple thou hast none,
      Nor altar heap'd with flowers;
Nor virgin-choir to make delicious moan
      Upon the midnight hours;
No voice, no lute, no pipe, no incense sweet
   From chain-swung censer teeming;
No shrine, no grove, no oracle, no heat
   Of pale-mouth'd prophet dreaming.

O brightest! though too late for antique vows,
   Too, too late for the fond believing lyre,
When holy were the haunted forest boughs,
   Holy the air, the water, and the fire;
Yet even in these days so far retir'd
   From happy pieties, thy lucent fans,
   Fluttering among the faint Olympians,
I see, and sing, by my own eyes inspir'd.
So let me be thy choir, and make a moan
       Upon the midnight hours;
Thy voice, thy lute, thy pipe, thy incense sweet
   From swinged censer teeming;
Thy shrine, thy grove, thy oracle, thy heat
   Of pale-mouth'd prophet dreaming.

Yes, I will be thy priest, and build a fane
   In some untrodden region of my mind,
Where branched thoughts, new grown with pleasant pain,
   Instead of pines shall murmur in the wind:
Far, far around shall those dark-cluster'd trees
   Fledge the wild-ridged mountains steep by steep;
And there by zephyrs, streams, and birds, and bees,
   The moss-lain Dryads shall be lull'd to sleep;
And in the midst of this wide quietness
A rosy sanctuary will I dress
With the wreath'd trellis of a working brain,
   With buds, and bells, and stars without a name,
With all the gardener Fancy e'er could feign,
   Who breeding flowers, will never breed the same:
And there shall be for thee all soft delight
   That shadowy thought can win,
A bright torch, and a casement ope at night,
   To let the warm Love in!

Lines on the Mermaid Tavern

Souls of Poets dead and gone,
What Elysium have ye known,
Happy field or mossy cavern,
Choicer than the Mermaid Tavern?

Have ye tippled drink more fine
Than mine host's Canary wine?
Or are fruits of Paradise
Sweeter than those dainty pies
Of venison? O generous food!
Drest as though bold Robin Hood
Would, with his maid Marian,
Sup and bowse from horn and can.

　I have heard that on a day
Mine host's sign-board flew away,
Nobody knew whither, till
An astrologer's old quill
To a sheepskin gave the story,
Said he saw you in your glory,
Underneath a new old sign
Sipping beverage divine,
And pledging with contented smack
The Mermaid in the Zodiac.

　Souls of Poets dead and gone,
What Elysium have ye known,
Happy field or mossy cavern,
Choicer than the Mermaid Tavern?

To Autumn

I　Season of mists and mellow fruitfulness,
　　Close bosom-friend of the maturing sun;
Conspiring with him how to load and bless
　　With fruit the vines that round the thatch-eaves run;
To bend with apples the moss'd cottage-trees,
　　And fill all fruit with ripeness to the core;
　　　To swell the gourd, and plump the hazel shells
　　With a sweet kernel; to set budding more,
And still more, later flowers for the bees,
Until they think warm days will never cease,
　　　For Summer has o'er-brimm'd their clammy cells.

II　Who hath not seen thee oft amid thy store?
　　Sometimes whoever seeks abroad may find

Thee sitting careless on a granary floor,
   Thy hair soft-lifted by the winnowing wind;
Or on a half-reap'd furrow sound asleep,
    Drows'd with the fume of poppies, while thy hook
      Spares the next swath and all its twined flowers:
And sometimes like a gleaner thou dost keep
    Steady thy laden head across a brook;
    Or by a cyder-press, with patient look,
      Thou watchest the last oozings hours by hours.

III Where are the songs of Spring? Ay, where are they?
    Think not of them, thou hast thy music too, —
While barred clouds bloom the soft-dying day,
    And touch the stubble-plains with rosy hue;
Then in a wailful choir the small gnats mourn
    Among the river sallows, borne aloft
      Or sinking as the light wind lives or dies;
And full-grown lambs loud bleat from hilly bourn;
    Hedge-crickets sing; and now with treble soft
    The red-breast whistles from a garden-croft;
      And gathering swallows twitter in the skies.

Ode on Melancholy

I No, no, go not to Lethe, neither twist
    Wolf's-bane, tight-rooted, for its poisonous wine;
Nor suffer thy pale forehead to be kiss'd
    By nightshade, ruby grape of Proserpine;
Make not your rosary of yew-berries,
    Nor let the beetle, nor the death-moth be
      Your mournful Psyche, nor the downy owl
A partner in your sorrow's mysteries;
    For shade to shade will come too drowsily,
      And drown the wakeful anguish of the soul.

II But when the melancholy fit shall fall
    Sudden from heaven like a weeping cloud,
That fosters the droop-headed flowers all,
    And hides the green hill in an April shroud;
Then glut thy sorrow on a morning rose,
    Or on the rainbow of the salt sand-wave,

Or on the wealth of globed peonies;
Or if thy mistress some rich anger shows,
    Emprison her soft hand, and let her rave,
        And feed deep, deep upon her peerless eyes.

III   She dwells with Beauty — Beauty that must die;
    And Joy, whose hand is ever at his lips
Bidding adieu; and aching Pleasure nigh,
    Turning to Poison while the bee-mouth sips:
Ay, in the very temple of delight
    Veil'd Melancholy has her sovran shrine,
        Though seen of none save him whose strenuous tongue
Can burst Joy's grape against his palate fine;
His soul shall taste the sadness of her might,
    And be among her cloudy trophies hung.

La Belle Dame sans Merci

A BALLAD

I   O, what can ail thee, knight-at-arms,
        Alone and palely loitering?
    The sedge has wither'd from the lake,
        And no birds sing.

II   O, what can ail thee, knight-at-arms,
        So haggard and so woe-begone?
    The squirrel's granary is full,
        And the harvest's done.

III   I see a lilly on thy brow,
        With anguish moist and fever dew;
    And on thy cheeks a fading rose
        Fast withereth too.

IV   I met a lady in the meads,
        Full beautiful — a faery's child,
    Her hair was long, her foot was light,
        And her eyes were wild.

V   I made a garland for her head,
      And bracelets too, and fragrant zone;
    She look'd at me as she did love,
      And made sweet moan.

VI   I set her on my pacing steed,
      And nothing else saw all day long;
    For sidelong would she bend, and sing
      A faery's song.

VII   She found me roots of relish sweet,
      And honey wild, and manna dew,
    And sure in language strange she said —
      'I love thee true'.

VIII   She took me to her elfin grot,
      And there she wept and sigh'd full sore,
    And there I shut her wild wild eyes
      With kisses four.

IX   And there she lulled me asleep
      And there I dream'd — Ah! woe betide!
    The latest dream I ever dream'd
      On the cold hill side.

X   I saw pale kings and princes too,
      Pale warriors, death-pale were they all;
    They cried — 'La Belle Dame sans Merci
      Hath thee in thrall!'

XI   I saw their starved lips in the gloam,
      With horrid warning gaped wide,
    And I awoke and found me here,
      On the cold hill's side.

XII   And this is why I sojourn here
      Alone and palely loitering,
    Though the sedge has wither'd from the lake,
      And no birds sing.

Ode on Indolence

'They toil not, neither do they spin.'

I   One morn before me were three figures seen,
        With bowed necks, and joined hands, side-faced;
    And one behind the other stepp'd serene,
        In placid sandals, and in white robes graced;
    They pass'd, like figures on a marble urn,
        When shifted round to see the other side;
            They came again; as when the urn once more
    Is shifted round, the first seen shades return;
        And they were strange to me, as may betide
            With vases, to one deep in Phidian lore.

II   How is it, Shadows! that I knew ye not?
        How came ye muffled in so hush a mask?
    Was it a silent deep-disguised plot
        To steal away, and leave without a task
    My idle days? Ripe was the drowsy hour;
        The blissful cloud of summer-indolence
            Benumb'd my eyes; my pulse grew less and less;
    Pain had no sting, and pleasure's wreath no flower:
        O, why did ye not melt, and leave my sense
            Unhaunted quite of all but — nothingness?

III A third time came they by; — alas! wherefore?
        My sleep had been embroider'd with dim dreams;
    My soul had been a lawn besprinkled o'er
        With flowers, and stirring shades, and baffled beams.
    The morn was clouded, but no shower fell,
        Tho' in her lids hung the sweet tears of May;
            The open casement press'd a new-leav'd vine,
        Let in the budding warmth and throstle's lay;
    O Shadows! 'twas a time to bid farewell!
        Upon your skirts had fallen no tears of mine.

IV   A third time pass'd they by, and, passing, turn'd
        Each one the face a moment whiles to me;

Then faded, and to follow them I burn'd
    And ach'd for wings because I knew the three;
The first was a fair Maid, and Love her name;
    The second was Ambition, pale of cheek,
      And ever watchful with fatigued eye;
The last, whom I love more, the more of blame
    Is heap'd upon her, maiden most unmeek, —
      I knew to be my demon Poesy.

V They faded, and, forsooth! I wanted wings:
    O folly! What is love! and where is it?
And for that poor Ambition! it springs
    From a man's little heart's short fever-fit;
For Poesy! — no, — she has not a joy, —
    At least for me, — so sweet as drowsy noons,
      And evenings steep'd in honied indolence;
O, for an age so shelter'd from annoy,
    That I may never know how change the moons,
      Or hear the voice of busy common-sense!

VI So, ye Three Ghosts, adieu! Ye cannot raise
    My head cool-bedded in the flowery grass;
For I would not be dieted with praise,
    A pet-lamb in a sentimental farce!
Fade softly from my eyes, and be once more
    In masque-like figures on the dreamy urn;
      Farewell! I yet have visions for the night,
And for the day faint visions there is store;
      Vanish, ye Phantoms! from my idle spright,
    Into the clouds, and never more return!

On the Sea

It keeps eternal whisperings around
    Desolate shores, and with its mighty swell
    Gluts twice ten thousand Caverns, till the spell
Of Hecate leaves them their old shadowy sound.

Often 'tis in such gentle temper found,
    That scarcely will the very smallest shell
    Be mov'd for days from where it sometime fell,
When last the winds of Heaven were unbound.
Oh ye! who have your eye-balls vex'd and tir'd,
    Feast them upon the wideness of the Sea;
        Oh ye! whose ears are dinn'd with uproar rude,
    Or fed too much with cloying melody —
        Sit ye near some old Cavern's Mouth and brood,
Until ye start, as if the sea-nymphs quir'd!

"When I have fears that I may cease to be"

When I have fears that I may cease to be
    Before my pen has glean'd my teeming brain,
Before high-piled books, in charactery,
    Hold like rich garners the full ripen'd grain;
When I behold, upon the night's starr'd face,
    Huge cloudy symbols of a high romance,
And think that I may never live to trace
    Their shadows, with the magic hand of chance;
And when I feel, fair creature of an hour,
    That I shall never look upon thee more,
Never have relish in the faery power
    Of unreflecting love; — then on the shore
Of the wide world I stand alone, and think
Till love and fame to nothingness do sink.

To Homer

Standing aloof in giant ignorance,
    Of thee I hear and of the Cyclades,
As one who sits ashore and longs perchance
    To visit dolphin-coral in deep seas.
So thou wast blind; — but then the veil was rent,
    For Jove uncurtain'd Heaven to let thee live,
And Neptune made for thee a spumy tent,
    And Pan made sing for thee his forest-hive;
Aye on the shores of darkness there is light,
    And precipices show untrodden green,
There is a budding morrow in midnight,

There is a triple sight in blindness keen;
Such seeing hadst thou, as it once befel
To Dian, Queen of Earth, and Heaven, and Hell.

To Sleep

O soft embalmer of the still midnight,
    Shutting, with careful fingers and benign,
Our gloom-pleas'd eyes, embower'd from the light,
    Enshaded in forgetfulness divine:
O soothest Sleep! if so it please thee, close
    In midst of this thine hymn my willing eyes,
Or wait the amen, ere thy poppy throws
    Around my bed its lulling charities.
Then save me, or the passed day will shine
Upon my pillow, breeding many woes, —
    Save me from curious Conscience, that still lords
Its strength for darkness, burrowing like a mole;
    Turn the key deftly in the oiled wards,
And seal the hushed Casket of my Soul.

"Why did I laugh to-night? . . ."

Why did I laugh to-night? No voice will tell:
    No God, no Demon of severe response,
Deigns to reply from Heaven or from Hell.
    Then to my human heart I turn at once.
Heart! Thou and I are here sad and alone;
    I say, why did I laugh! O mortal pain!
O Darkness! Darkness! ever must I moan,
    To question Heaven and Hell and Heart in vain.
Why did I laugh? I know this Being's lease,
    My fancy to its utmost blisses spreads;
Yet would I on this very midnight cease,
    And the world's gaudy ensigns see in shreds;
Verse, Fame, and Beauty are intense indeed,
But Death intenser — Death is Life's high meed.

"Bright star, . . ."

Bright star, would I were stedfast as thou art —
    Not in lone splendour hung aloft the night

And watching, with eternal lids apart,
    Like nature's patient, sleepless Eremite,
The moving waters at their priestlike task
    Of pure ablution round earth's human shores,
Or gazing on the new soft-fallen mask
    Of snow upon the mountains and the moors —
No — yet still stedfast, still unchangeable,
    Pillow'd upon my fair love's ripening breast,
To feel for ever its soft fall and swell,
    Awake for ever in a sweet unrest,
Still, still to hear her tender-taken breath,
And so live ever — or else swoon to death.

On seeing the Elgin Marbles

My spirit is too weak — mortality
    Weighs heavily on me like unwilling sleep,
    And each imagin'd pinnacle and steep
Of godlike hardship, tells me I must die
Like a sick Eagle looking at the sky.
    Yet 'tis a gentle luxury to weep
    That I have not the cloudy winds to keep,
Fresh for the opening of the morning's eye.
Such dim-conceived glories of the brain
    Bring round the heart an undescribable feud;
So do these wonders a most dizzy pain,
    That mingles Grecian grandeur with the rude
Wasting of old Time — with a billowy main —
    A sun — a shadow of a magnitude.

To J. H. Reynolds Esq.

Dear Reynolds! as last night I lay in bed,
There came before my eyes that wonted thread
Of shapes, and shadows, and remembrances,
That every other minute vex and please:
Things all disjointed come from north and south, —
Two Witch's eyes above a Cherub's mouth,

Voltaire with casque and shield and habergeon,
And Alexander with his nightcap on;
Old Socrates a-tying his cravat,
And Hazlitt playing with Miss Edgeworth's cat;
And Junius Brutus, pretty well so so,
Making the best of's way towards Soho.

Few are there who escape these visitings, —
Perhaps one or two whose lives have patent wings,
And thro' whose curtains peeps no hellish nose,
No wild-boar tushes, and no Mermaid's toes;
But flowers bursting out with lusty pride,
And young Æolian harps personified;
Some Titian colours touch'd into real life, —
The sacrifice goes on; the pontiff knife
Gleams in the Sun, the milk-white heifer lows,
The pipes go shrilly, the libation flows:
A white sail shows above the green-head cliff,
Moves round the point, and throws her anchor stiff;
The mariners join hymn with those on land.

You know the Enchanted Castle, — it doth stand
Upon a rock, on the border of a Lake,
Nested in trees, which all do seem to shake
From some old magic like Urganda's Sword.
O Phœbus! that I had thy sacred word
To show this Castle, in fair dreaming wise,
Unto my friend, while sick and ill he lies!

You know it well enough, where it doth seem
A mossy place, a Merlin's Hall, a dream;
You know the clear Lake, and the little Isles,
The mountains blue, and cold near neighbour rills,
All which elsewhere are but half animate;
There do they look alive to love and hate,
To smiles and frowns; they seem a lifted mound
Above some giant, pulsing underground.

Part of the Building was a chosen See,
Built by a banish'd Santon of Chaldee;
The other part, two thousand years from him,
Was built by Cuthbert de Saint Aldebrim;

Then there's a little wing, far from the Sun,
Built by a Lapland Witch turn'd maudlin Nun;
And many other juts of aged stone
Founded with many a mason-devil's groan.

   The doors all look as if they op'd themselves,
The windows as if latch'd by Fays and Elves,
And from them comes a silver flash of light,
As from the westward of a Summer's night;
Or like a beauteous woman's large blue eyes
Gone mad thro' olden songs and poesies.

   See! what is coming from the distance dim!
A golden Galley all in silken trim!
Three rows of oars are lightening, moment whiles,
Into the verd'rous bosoms of those isles;
Towards the shade, under the Castle wall,
It comes in silence, — now 'tis hidden all.
The Clarion sounds, and from a Postern-gate
An echo of sweet music doth create
A fear in the poor Herdsman, who doth bring
His beasts to trouble the enchanted spring, —
He tells of the sweet music, and the spot,
To all his friends, and they believe him not.

   O that our dreamings all, of sleep or wake,
Would all their colours from the sunset take:
From something of material sublime,
Rather than shadow our own soul's day-time
In the dark void of night. For in the world
We jostle, — but my flag is not unfurl'd
On the Admiral-staff, — and so philosophize
I dare not yet! Oh, never will the prize,
High reason, and the love of good and ill,
Be my award! Things cannot to the will
Be settled, but they tease us out of thought;
Or is it that imagination brought
Beyond its proper bound, yet still confin'd,
Lost in a sort of Purgatory blind,
Cannot refer to any standard law
Of either earth or heaven? It is a flaw

In happiness, to see beyond our bourn, —
It forces us in summer skies to mourn,
It soils the singing of the Nightingale.

 Dear Reynolds! I have a mysterious tale,
And cannot speak it: the first page I read
Upon a Lampit rock of green sea-weed
Among the breakers; 'twas a quiet eve,
The rocks were silent, the wide sea did weave
An untumultuous fringe of silver foam
Along the flat brown sand; I was at home
And should have been most happy, — but I saw
Too far into the sea, where every maw
The greater on the less feeds evermore. —
But I saw too distinct into the core
Of an eternal fierce destruction,
And so from happiness I far was gone.
Still am I sick of it, and tho', to-day,
I've gather'd young spring-leaves, and flowers gay
Of periwinkle and wild strawberry,
Still do I that most fierce destruction see, —
The Shark at savage prey, — the Hawk at pounce, —
The gentle Robin, like a Pard or Ounce,
Ravening a worm, — Away, ye horrid moods!
Moods of one's mind! You know I hate them well.
You know I'd sooner be a clapping Bell
To some Kamtschatcan Missionary Church,
Than with these horrid moods be left i' the lurch.

To Mrs. Reynolds's Cat

Cat! who hast pass'd thy grand climacteric,
 How many mice and rats hast in thy days
  Destroy'd? — How many tit bits stolen? Gaze
With those bright languid segments green, and prick
Those velvet ears — but pr'ythee do not stick
 Thy latent talons in me — and uppraise
  Thy gentle mew — and tell me all thy frays
Of fish and mice, and rats and tender chick.

Nay, look not down, nor lick thy dainty wrists —
  For all the wheezy asthma, — and for all
Thy tail's tip is nick'd off — and though the fists
  Of many a maid have given thee many a maul,
Still is that fur as soft as when the lists
  In youth thou enter'dst on glass-bottled wall.

Alphabetical List of Titles and First Lines